Drama Clas

The Drama Classics s
plays in affordable paperback ~~cucum~~
and theatregoers. The hallmarks of the series are accessible
introductions, uncluttered texts and an overall theatrical
perspective.

Given that readers may be encountering a particular play for
the first time, the introduction seeks to fill in the theatrical/
historical background and to outline the chief themes rather
than concentrate on interpretational and textual analysis.
Similarly the play-texts themselves are free of footnotes and
other interpolations: instead there is an end-glossary of
'difficult' words and phrases.

The texts of the English-language plays in the series
have been prepared taking full account of all existing
scholarship. The foreign-language plays have been newly
translated into a modern English that is both actable and
accurate: many of the translators regularly have their work
staged professionally.

Edited until his early death by Kenneth McLeish, the Drama
Classics series continues with his aim of providing a first-class
library of dramatic literature representing the best of world
theatre.

Associate editor:
Professor Trevor R. Griffiths
School of Arts and Humanities
University of North London

DRAMA CLASSICS *the first hundred*

The Alchemist
All for Love
Andromache
Antigone
Arden of Faversham
Bacchae
Bartholomew Fair
The Beaux Stratagem
The Beggar's Opera
Birds
The Broken Jug
The Changeling
The Cherry Orchard
Children of the Sun
El Cid
The Country Wife
Cyrano de Bergerac
The Dance of Death
The Devil is an Ass
Doctor Faustus
A Doll's House
Don Juan
The Duchess of
    Malfi
Edward II
Electra (Euripides)
Electra (Sophocles)
An Enemy of the
    People
The Eunuch
Every Man in his
    Humour
Everyman
The Father
Faust
A Flea in her Ear
Frogs
Fuenteovejuna
The Game of Love
    and Chance

Ghosts
The Government
    Inspector
Hedda Gabler
The Hypochondriac
The Importance of
    Being Earnest
An Ideal Husband
An Italian Straw Hat
The Jew of Malta
The Lady from the Sea
The Learned Ladies
Life is a Dream
The Lower Depths
The Lucky Chance
Lulu
Lysistrata
The Magistrate
The Malcontent
The Man of Mode
The Marriage of Figaro
Mary Stuart
The Master Builder
Medea
Menaechmi
The Misanthrope
The Miser
Miss Julie
A Month in the
    Country
A New Way to Pay Old
    Debts
Oedipus at Kolonos
Oedipus the King
The Oresteia
Peer Gynt
Phaedra
Philoctetes
The Playboy of the
    Western World

The Recruiting
    Officer
The Revenger's
    Tragedy
The Rivals
The Robbers
La Ronde
Rosmersholm
The Rover
The School for
    Scandal
The Seagull
The Servant of Two
    Masters
She Stoops to
    Conquer
The Shoemaker's
    Holiday
The Spanish Tragedy
Spring's Awakening
Tartuffe
Thérèse Raquin
Three Sisters
'Tis Pity She's a Whore
Too Clever by Half
Ubu
Uncle Vanya
Vassa Zheleznova
Volpone
The Way of the World
The White Devil
The Wild Duck
Women Beware
    Women
Women of Troy
Woyzeck

*The publishers welcome
suggestions for further titles*

DRAMA CLASSICS

THE JEW OF MALTA

by

Christopher Marlowe

edited and introduced by
Peter J. Smith

NICK HERN BOOKS
London

A Drama Classic

This edition of *The Jew of Malta* first published in Great Britain as a paperback original in 1994 by Nick Hern Books Limited, 14 Larden Road, London W3 7ST

Reprinted 1999

Copyright in the edition of the text © 1994 by Peter J. Smith
Copyright in the introduction © 1994 Nick Hern Books Ltd

Typeset by Country Setting, Kingsdown, Kent CT14 8ES
Printed in Great Britain by Bath Press, Avon

A CIP catalogue record for this book is available from the British Library

ISBN 1 85459 199 1

Introduction

Christopher Marlowe (1564-93)

Marlowe was baptised in Canterbury on 26 February 1564, exactly two months before Shakespeare's christening in Stratford. He attended the King's School in Canterbury and Corpus Christi College, Cambridge. He received his B.A. in 1584 and his M.A. three years later. The second degree was insisted on by the Privy Council – and the intervention of so powerful a body, with its disclosure that Marlowe was employed 'in matters touching the benefit of his country', has been interpreted as evidence that he was working on sensitive government business. In 1587 he moved to London, achieving instant success with *Tamburlaine* and writing its sequel almost immediately. Two years later he was involved in a fatal sword-fight for which he was briefly imprisoned before being discharged.

On 12 May 1593, the playwright Thomas Kyd was arrested in possession of heretical documents. Kyd claimed that these papers belonged to Marlowe (with whom he had shared lodgings), and on 20 May Marlowe was ordered to report daily to the Privy Council. Ten days later, he met Ingram Frizer, Nicholas Skeres, and Robert Poley at a house in Deptford. During the meeting Marlowe was killed. Frizer (who was employed by Thomas Walsingham, a cousin of Sir Francis Walsingham, head of Elizabeth I's intelligence service) later claimed to have stabbed Marlowe in self-defence during an argument over the bill. At about the same time, a note was submitted to the authorities 'containing the opinion of one

Christopher Marly concerning his damnable judgment of religion and scorn of God's word'. The source of this blasphemous note was Richard Baines, an enemy of Marlowe and long-time agent of Walsingham. Marlowe – as befitted a blasphemer – was buried in an unmarked grave in Deptford, and one month later Frizer was officially pardoned. Whether Marlowe's death was the result of a spontaneous row, the outcome of factional intrigue, or because he was a spy who knew too much, remains a matter of speculation. Nothing in Marlowe's life immortalised him like the leaving of it. His death remains shrouded in intrigue – itself the subject of an increasing number of novels and plays.

The Jew of Malta: **What Happens in the Play**

Ferneze, Governor of Malta, has allowed the island's regular tribute to the Turks to fall ten years in arrears. Selim-Calymath, son of the Turkish Emperor, grants Ferneze one month to find the money, and the Governor decrees that the Jews of the island will have to pay the entire sum; if they refuse, they will be forced to become Christians. When Barabas objects to this, his goods are seized and his house is converted into a nunnery. He persuades his daughter Abigail to feign conversion to Catholicism; she will then be able to enter the house and recover some money he has hidden beneath the floorboards.

Barabas uses the recovered money to buy an evil servant, Ithamore, who will assist him in his revenge. He promises his daughter to both Don Lodowick (Ferneze's son) and Don Mathias (with whom Abigail is in fact in love), and employs Ithamore to stir up trouble between them by carrying each a faked challenge from his rival. The two men stab each other, and Abigail, heartbroken at Mathias's death, genuinely converts to Christianity and enters the nunnery. Outraged by this, Barabas, with characteristic extremism, kills all the nuns with poisoned porridge. While all this is going on, the prostitute

Bellamira seduces Ithamore while her pimp, Pilia-Borza, encourages him to blackmail Barabas. Disguised as a French musician, Barabas offers all three a bouquet of poisoned flowers but they survive just long enough to inform Ferneze of the murders he has organised, including that of the Governor's own son. Before Barabas can be executed, he feigns death by taking a sleeping draught and his body is thrown over the walls of the town 'to be a prey for vultures and wild beasts'.

When Barabas awakes, he offers his services to the invading Turks, leading them into the town through the sewers, and they surprise and arrest Ferneze. At this point Barabas seriously miscalculates by offering, in return for a fee, to reinstate Ferneze as Governor of Malta and entrap Calymath's soldiers. The Governor agrees; the soldiers are blown up; Ferneze then double-crosses Barabas and he ends up in the boiling cauldron intended for Calymath. The Governor is restored to power and holds Calymath as a hostage until his father agrees to compensate Malta. Ferneze's opportunism is sanctimoniously revealed in the final ironic lines of the play in which he attributes his victory to God's will: 'So march away, and let due praise be given / Neither to Fate nor Fortune, but to Heaven.'

Marlowe the Dramatist

Marlowe was a Latin scholar, and the Dido and Aeneas story from Virgil's epic poem *The Aeneid* was one of his first pieces of dramatic writing. Seeking an English equivalent for Virgil's rolling hexameters, he perfected what came to be called 'blank verse' – and revealed its full potential some three years later in *Tamburlaine*, where poetry all but engulfs plot, characterisation and narrative structure. This works well in *Tamburlaine*, which is essentially an epic poem for the stage rather than a play; and Marlowe's 'mighty line' (as Jonson later called it) set a style and a standard for Elizabethan epic drama.

In *The Jew of Malta* Marlowe imported a technique almost totally missing in *Tamburlaine* (or indeed in Virgil): dramatic irony. Characters consistently play against type and against expectation, and our enjoyment depends as much on what we know or suspect as on what we see. Barabas is a darkly comic figure, derived less from Roman sources than from the saturnine Tempters of English medieval drama. He is the ancestor of a whole range of such characters in later drama, not least such Shakespearean creations as Aaron in *Titus Andronicus*, King John and – perhaps most dazzling of all – Richard III. Ambivalence and comic vitality were fresh qualities in 1580s English drama, and they, no less than the 'mighty line', were Marlowe's main contributions to the art.

Original Staging

The Jew of Malta was probably first staged by an acting company known as Strange's Men (after their patron, Lord Strange), led by the great actor Edward Alleyn (1566-1626). Alleyn, as well as being the creator of Marlowe's tragic heroes, became one of the period's leading theatrical entrepreneurs in partnership with his father-in-law, Philip Henslowe (died 1616).

Elizabethan theatres such as the Rose, which Henslowe built in 1587, offered sophisticated playing spaces for performances which were watched by a wide cross-section of Elizabethan society. Theatres were usually circular or polygonal. The basic admission price allowed a spectator to stand in a yard open to the weather around a raised stage thrust out from a wall of the theatre. Surrounding the yard were galleries with seating for spectators who had paid an additional entrance fee. The wall behind the stage housed the dressing rooms (known as the tiring house), and actors entered and exited through doors in the tiring house wall. There was a gallery above the stage, which was probably used for various purposes: as a way of staging scenes that required an upper level, or as an exclusive audience space, or perhaps as a musicians' gallery. As Act Five of *The Jew of Malta* suggests, properties could be winched down from the 'heavens' (the name given to the covering over the stage). There were also trapdoors in the stage floor.

Elizabethan theatre was not concerned with presenting an illusion of reality: there was no realistic scenery or accurate historical costuming in the modern sense, and the action moved fluidly across the unlocalised stage. Performances took place in the afternoon in natural light, and furniture and large properties were set and removed as required in full view of the audience. A scene's time and location could be established verbally or through the use of props: a throne might indicate a palace, and night might be suggested with torches, as in Act Two of *The Jew of Malta*. And, although the effects of this are hotly debated, all parts were played by male actors, with women's roles being played by young apprentices. The large casts used in most Elizabethan plays would have required extensive doubling of the minor parts.

Niccolò Machiavelli (1469-1527)

Many Elizabethans must have viewed Machiavelli's *The Prince* in the same way as Salman Rushdie's *The Satanic Verses* is today by its Muslim opponents. In both cases the author is perceived as a blasphemous monster and the book that arouses this reputation is often unread by its adversaries. Ironically, a modern reader may well find a perverse appeal in *The Prince*'s candid mixture of brutality and *realpolitik*, compared with the disingenuousness of modern political corruption. Machiavelli's ideal Prince is a political actor performing the role of a sincere and virtuous ruler. He insists upon the cultivation, in the absence of religious conviction, of a religious persona:

> it is not necessary for a prince to have all of the above-mentioned qualities, [wisdom, goodness, piety, honour]

but it is very necessary for him to appear to have them. Furthermore, I shall be so bold as to assert this: that having them and practising them at all times is harmful; and appearing to have them is useful; for instance, to seem merciful, faithful, humane, trustworthy, religious.

The Prince, ed. Peter Bondanella (Oxford, 1984), p. 59

Although Machiavelli's manifesto was not translated into English until 1640, his reputation as the foremost apologist for political ruthlessness and treachery was secured many years before, partly because of vehement reactions from English and French opponents and partly as a result of the hysterical mythologising of his justification of power. Marlowe's contribution to the demonisation of Machiavelli is made clear at the beginning of *The Jew of Malta.* In the play's prologue, Machevill ('make evil') dismisses all his enemies in a way designed to prepare us for the unashamed double-dealing of Barabas: 'let them know that I am Machevill, / And weigh not men, and therefore not men's words'. With a mixture of bravado and nonchalance, Machevill rubbishes the arguments of his opponents and introduces his disciple to an audience who would then see Barabas as the incarnation of the insidious principles of this Italianate bogeyman.

Marlowe's 'Machevill' emphasises the 'evil' in Machiavelli's name; it was also no accident that 'Old Nick', for the Elizabethans, was an alias of the Devil. As late as 1611, John Davies was still playing with the name, writing in his *Scourge of Folly* of '*Mach-evil* that *evil* none can match' and noting that the '*Machia-villain* [is] in a sheep-skin clad, the wolf or fox.' For many Elizabethans, Machiavelli was a wolf in sheep's clothing. To Marlowe, by contrast, his may have seemed the voice of a dangerous new modernity – ruthless, secular, and eminently dramatic.

Racism and Jewishness

The fact that we tend to view Renaissance literature as 'classic'
can lead us to excuse or ignore less savoury aspects of plays like
The Jew of Malta or Shakespeare's *The Merchant of Venice*. In the
aftermath of the industrialised slaughter of the Jews
perpetrated by the Nazis, it is certainly difficult to view a play
like *The Jew of Malta* as being entirely harmless. Barry Kyle,
who directed it for the Royal Shakespeare Company in 1987,
expressed his misgivings about the issues raised by its staging:

> I read *The Jew of Malta* when I was a student and thought it
> was unrevivable. I find the whole issue of anti-semitic drama
> and whether you should revive it very difficult. I've actually
> directed *The Merchant of Venice* in Israel, so I've been through
> this discussion at some length. It was quite influential on the
> thinking I had in *The Jew of Malta*. I couldn't bear the idea
> of it seeming to be an anti-semitic piece of work.
>
> *This Golden Round: The Royal Shakespeare Company at the Swan,*
> ed. Ronnie Mulryne and Margaret Shewring
> (Stratford-upon-Avon, 1989), p. 75

Kyle's *Jew of Malta* was in fact an anti-Christian production of
an anti-Semitic text. It opposed a witty and adroit Alun
Armstrong as Barabas against a ruthless and hard-faced John
Carlisle as Ferneze, and left us in no doubt as to who the real
villain was. At the opening, Machevill's prologue was spoken
from a trapeze in a savage mock-Italian drawl. At the end of
the play, as the trapeze, which had just lowered Barabas into
the boiling cauldron, was raised from the trapdoor, Ferneze
stepped onto it to give his last speech – and at the lines: 'So,
march away, and let due praise be given / Neither to Fate
nor Fortune, but to Heaven', he pulled off his wig to reveal
Machevill's black hair, and once again used the accent of the
opening prologue. The real Machevill, the production thus
assured us, was not the wicked Jew, but the scheming and
successful Christian Governor.

Kyle's production showed that reading the play against its own anti-Semitic grain is one way to continue to stage it and avoid the charge of racism. But this saving of the appearances has not always been possible. By 1564, the year of Marlowe's birth, Jews had been officially banned from England for almost three hundred years. England had been the first country to enforce the compulsory wearing of the yellow badge and, following a series of massacres, had expelled the entire Jewish population from its national territory. Literature in the middle ages repeatedly associates its stock Vice/Jew figure with Satan, and the Jews are held directly responsible for the death of Christ. Stories of infanticide and child crucifixion were commonplace in the middle ages and the early modern period. When Barnadine, in this play, tells Jacomo that he has something 'to exclaim against the Jew', his fellow friar replies, 'What, has he crucified a child?' Elsewhere in the play, Barabas describes 'standard' Jewish cruelty to Ithamore: it includes the killing of 'sick people groaning under walls' and the poisoning of wells. He goes on to describe his sadistic way of living:

> Then after that was I an usurer,
> And with extorting, cozening, forfeiting,
> And tricks belonging unto brokery,
> I filled the jails with bankrouts in a year,
> And with young orphans planted hospitals,
> And every moon made some or other mad,
> And now and then one hang himself for grief,
> Pinning upon his breast a long great scroll
> How I with interest tormented him.

The 'interest' with which Barabas torments his victims refers not only to the amounts of profit that result from loan-sharking but to the relish with which the spiteful usurer conducts his affairs. Jews were particularly associated with sadistic financial dealings. Credit and money-lending were outlawed by the Christian Church and the sinfulness of usury was connected with God's curse upon Adam: Francis Bacon, in his essay 'Of Usury', notes that men were condemned to produce food in the sweat of their own brows, not in that of their neighbour. Money-lending was a mortal sin, but since Jews were supposed to be going to Hell anyway, it didn't matter that they dabbled in it. The common pun on use and *Jews (iuse)*, making money-lending the trade of this religious and racial group, supported the argument that because the Jews were supposedly wealthy, they ought to be made to pay more tax. In Marlowe's play, Ferneze's decree ensures that racial discrimination forms just such a basis for paying the Turkish tribute, which 'shall all be levied amongst the Jews, and each of them to pay one half of his estate'.

The Title

It is sometimes argued that because there was no open Jewish community to form the target of anti-Semitism at the time when Marlowe wrote, *The Jew of Malta* cannot be racist. This fails to acknowledge that there is a causal relationship between anti-Semitic propaganda and anti-Semitic violence, and it also overlooks the importance of the title of the play itself. Marlowe's other major plays centre dramatically on a main character, and the titles of the plays coincide with their central protagonists: *Tamburlaine, Dr Faustus, Edward II*. But this play is not called *Barabas*. The reason may be that Marlowe is more interested in exploiting a stereotype of Jewishness than in exploring an individual. This preference for labelling Barabas a Jew before portraying him as a fully characterised individual is borne out by the play. Machevill says that he comes 'to present the tragedy of a Jew' but never names him. Later, when Barabas instructs the merchant to pay the customs duties with his credit, he describes himself as the Jew of Malta before giving his name: 'Go tell 'em the Jew of Malta sent thee, man: / Tush, who amongst 'em knows not Barabas?' Abigail identifies herself to the Abbess as 'The hopeless daughter of a hapless Jew, / The

Jew of Malta, wretched Barabas'. Repeatedly throughout the play, Barabas is a rich Jew *before* he is man, merchant, bourgeois figure, or father. Even when he is named, it is after the person for whom Christ most immediately died, the criminal who was pardoned so that Christ could be crucified in his place – a fact of which, as the note by Richard Baines protests, Marlowe was gleefully aware, since he is alleged to have held the opinion 'That Christ deserved better to die than Barabbas and that the Jews made a good choice though Barabbas were both a thief and a murderer.' The choice of character name underlines the charge of deicide levelled at all Jews in Marlowe's time.

The Jew of Malta and *The Merchant of Venice*

Nowadays, Marlowe's play is often read as a dramatic precursor of Shakespeare's *Merchant of Venice*. (Shakespeare may even have acted in *The Jew of Malta* in the early 1590s.) In terms of plot the two plays are strikingly alike. In each an isolated Jew exists within a morally dubious Christian society, and the plays explore, through interrelated themes of wealth, political power and geographical range, the tensions thrown up by such a relationship. In each case the Jew is accompanied by a servant, who leaves him (Gobbo) or betrays him (Ithamore). Both Jews' families are represented by a single daughter and in both cases the desire of this daughter to marry 'out' causes a rift between generations. The final downfall takes place in the teeth of political triumph. Barabas has been given the governorship of Malta and victory over Ferneze, while the Duke and Portia have granted Shylock's legal suit. Barabas is physically destroyed, while Shylock's humiliation, confiscation of his property, and compulsory religious conversion are represented as a fate worse than death.

The differences between the plays may appear even more spectacular. Structurally, for instance, Marlowe's play has neither an alternative setting that corresponds to Shakespeare's

Belmont nor any subplot corresponding to the confusion over the rings. But more important is the difference in the relationships between, on the one hand, Barabas and Malta, and, on the other, Shylock and Venice. Shakespeare refocuses the structure of Marlowe's play, making the actions of the Jew contingent upon those of his society as a whole. Barabas is largely successful in maintaining his independence; he has no loyalties and therefore no friends. He divides his enemies and inflames their mutual hatred, turning Turk against Christian and betraying Christian to Turk. He repeatedly resorts to role-playing, disguising himself as a French lute player, feigning death, pretending to lament his loss of wealth (when in fact he has coins hidden under a floorboard), and publicly scorning his daughter's mock-apostasy so that she can recover his booty. He is also quite prepared to betray the trust of his fellow-Jews. Debating their corporate action in the face of their unreasonable financial burden, he assures them 'If anything shall there concern our state, / Assure yourselves I'll look (*Aside*) unto myself'. Shakespeare's Shylock, by contrast, is solidly and faithfully Jewish. Although he does not have the money himself, he is confident that 'Tubal (a wealthy Hebrew of my tribe) / Will furnish me'. One is tempted to suggest that had Shylock approached Barabas for the loan, the latter would have pretended not to have been at home.

Religion: Faith or a 'Childish Toy'?

Another fundamental difference between *The Jew of Malta* and *The Merchant of Venice* concerns the attitude towards religious faith. Shylock regards his religion seriously. He is firm in his religious observance, as Barabas would never be. He is loyal to other Jews, and desirous that Jessica should marry one. In the courtroom scene, he imbues his 'bond' with the vehemence of religiosity: 'And by our holy Sabbath have I sworn / To have the due and forfeit of my bond.' In contrast, Barabas's pursuit of his religion is conducted in line with Machevill's conviction expressed in the prologue: 'I count religion but a childish toy, / And hold there is no sin but ignorance' – an assertion that chimes unfortunately with the opinion attributed toMarlowe by Richard Baines (see page vi) 'That the first beginning of religion was only to keep men in awe.'

In *The Prince* Machiavelli insisted that when political advantage required, virtuous principles should be abandoned. Barabas tells his daughter that it is morally acceptable to disguise herself as a nun 'for religion / Hides many mischiefs from suspicion'. In fact everybody on Malta works out their machinations under the guise of religious protestation. Ferneze justifies the imposition of the tax on the grounds that the guilt of the Jews has somehow brought it about in the first place: 'through our sufferance of your hateful lives / (Who stand accursed in the sight of Heaven) / These taxes and afflictions are befallen'. The running smut about the lewd behaviour of the nuns and the friars, which is confirmed in Act Three when Barnadine laments that Abigail has died a virgin, mocks the celibacy of Catholic orders. The ironies of religious hypocrisy are ever present. Ithamore remarks that 'To undo a Jew is charity, and not sin'; Barabas tells Abigail that 'It's no sin to deceive a Christian'. Religion is made a smoke-screen for political manipulation, and relationships, both familial and marital, mask a sinister interest in financial viability.

Marlowe Our Contemporary

In the fiercely materialistic world of Marlowe's play, a world in which people literally embody value and slaves have their price written on their backs, everybody is worth something. When Abigail rescues her father's coins in the Second Act, his rapturous jubilation oscillates between daughter and money: 'Oh girl, oh gold, oh beauty, oh my bliss!' Later, Barabas tells Lodowick that his daughter will be a diamond for his delight and possession. Personal integrity is continually treated as a commodity; every man – and, even more so, woman – has his/her price. In Act Four, in the course of his mock conversion, Barabas describes himself as 'a covetous wretch, / That would for lucre's sake have sold my soul.' The voracious materialism of the English Renaissance, shadowed in this play, expresses the aspirations of an age beginning to find its capitalistic feet – an age which looks bleakly forward to our own. *The Jew of Malta* is situated on the fault-line between an economy of ready cash on the one hand and the availability of credit on the other, dramatising what the critic James Shapiro recently called 'a cultural identity crisis'. The play's anti-Semitism is symptomatic of its particular historical position and the economic revolution taking place at the time. It is thus, mercifully, historically specific.

In the twentieth century, power struggles in Europe, Africa and elsewhere have given rise to such ghoulish euphemisms as 'the final solution', 'separate development' and 'ethnic cleansing'. Such terms have passed rather too readily into the language and are often used without their cautionary quotation marks. Now, more than ever, it may be time to divest Marlowe's text of its complacent and commonplace defences. *The Jew of Malta* can perhaps be fully understood only in the light of its historical specificity and its potentialities for racism.

Peter J. Smith
Northampton, 1994

'Marlowe the Dramatist' and 'Original Staging' by Kenneth McLeish and Trevor R. Griffiths

Note on the Text

The text printed here is based on the First Quarto, with spelling and punctuation regularised. All editorial additions appear within square brackets [like this].

For Further Reading

Harry Levin's *Christopher Marlowe: The Overreacher* (1952) remains a standard critical study. It considers the playwright as an incarnation of Icarus in myth and reads each of his protagonists as a version of this overreacher. Stephen Greenblatt's *Renaissance Self-Fashioning* (1980) contains an excellent essay on Marlowe in which he proposes that selves are constructed against and ultimately within external structures of power, through cycles of repetition. Roger Sales's study, *Christopher Marlowe* (1991) reads the plays within what he calls 'the dramatised nature of Elizabethan society', particularly the ritual violence of public execution. Sales is concerned to highlight the analogy between the implementation of power and its public display, demonstrating that power is itself a kind of theatrical performance.

Biographically, Charles Nicholl's *The Reckoning: The Murder of Christopher Marlowe* (1992) assembles a compelling narrative in favour of the conspiracy theory surrounding Marlowe's suspicious death and the involvement in it of government agents. Antony Burgess's novel *A Dead Man in Deptford* (1993) and Peter Whelan's play *The School of Night* (1992) offer their own interesting (and occasionally sensational) accounts.

Marlowe: Key Dates

1564   Born to John and Catherine Marlowe in Canterbury.
1584   B.A. awarded at Corpus Christi College, Cambridge.
        Before 1587, composition of *Dido, Queen of Carthage* (?)
1587   M.A. awarded on insistence of Privy Council. Moved
        to London. *Tamburlaine* produced.
1589   *The Jew of Malta* produced (?)
1592   *Edward II* produced (?) *Dr Faustus* produced (?)
        Tamburlaine published.
1593   *The Massacre at Paris* produced. Murdered by Ingram
        Frizer in Deptford. Authorities' receipt of 'the Baines
        note' accusing Marlowe of blasphemy and atheism.
1594   *Dido* and *Edward II* published.
1596   Translation of Ovid's *Elegies* published.
1598   *Hero and Leander* published.
1599   *The Passionate Pilgrim* published, containing Marlowe's
        lyric 'Come live with me and be my love'.
1600   Publication of *Lucan's First Book* and the anthology,
        England's Helicon containing 'Come live with me' and
        Ralegh's reply.
1604   Publication of *Dr Faustus* ('A text').
1616   Publication of *Dr Faustus* (in 'B text' with addition of
        comic scenes: interpolations of another playwright?).
1633   Publication of *The Jew of Malta* by the playwright
        Thomas Heywood.

The Prologue Spoken at Court

Gracious and great, that we so boldly dare
('Mongst other plays that now in fashion are)
To present this, writ many years agone,
And in that age thought second unto none,
We humbly crave your pardon. We pursue
The story of a rich and famous Jew
Who lived in Malta: you shall find him still,
In all his projects, a sound Machevill;
And that's his character. He that hath passed
So many censures is now come at last
To have your princely ears. Grace you him; then
You crown the action, and renown the pen.

Epilogue

It is our fear (dread Sovereign) we have been
Too tedious; neither can 't be less than sin
To wrong your princely patience. If we have,
(Thus low dejected) we your pardon crave;
And if aught here offend your ear or sight,
We only act and speak what others write.

THE JEW OF MALTA

[Dramatis Personae

MACHEVILL, the Prologue

BARABAS, the Jew

FERNEZE, a Governor of Malta

SELIM-CALYMATH, son to the Emperor of Turkey

Don MATHIAS, a gentleman } rivals for Abigail
Don LODOWICK, the Governor's son

Martin del BOSCO, the Spanish Vice-Admiral

ITHAMORE, a Turkish slave

JACOMO } friars
BARNARDINE

PILIA-BORZA, a pimp

Two MERCHANTS

Three JEWS

ABIGAIL, Barabas's daughter — *nunnery.*

KATHARINE, Mathias's mother

BELLAMIRA, a courtesan — *prostitute.*

ABBESS

A READER

NUNS, GOVERNORS, KNIGHTS, OFFICERS,
BASHAWS, TURKS, GUARD, SLAVES,
MESSENGER, CARPENTERS, ATTENDANTS]

EVENING STANDARD - THEATRE REVIEW.
The Jew of Malta → A complete
new insight into this fine play.

Imaginative & Canny.

[The Prologue]

MACHEVILL. Albeit the world think Machevill is dead,
    Yet was his soul but flown beyond the Alps,
    And now the Guise is dead, is come from France
    To view this land, and frolic with his friends.
    To some perhaps my name is odious,
    But such as love me, guard me from their tongues,
    And let them know that I am Machevill,
    And weigh not men, and therefore not men's words.
    Admired I am of those that hate me most.
    Though some speak openly against my books,   10
    Yet will they read me, and thereby attain
    To Peter's chair: and when they cast me off,
    Are poisoned by my climbing followers.
    I count religion but a childish toy,
    And hold there is no sin but ignorance.
    'Birds of the air will tell of murders past.'
    I am ashamed to hear such fooleries.
    Many will talk of title to a crown:
    What right had Caesar to the empire?
    Might first made kings, and laws were then most sure   20
    When like the Draco's they were writ in blood.
    Hence comes it, that a strong-built citadel
    Commands much more than letters can import:
    Which maxim had Phalaris observed,
    H' had never bellowed in a brazen bull
    Of great ones' envy; o'th'poor petty wits,

Let me be envied and not pitied!
But whither am I bound? I come not, I,
To read a lecture here in Britanie,
But to present the tragedy of a Jew   30
Who smiles to see how full his bags are crammed;
Which money was not got without my means.
I crave but this: grace him as he deserves,
And let him not be entertained the worse
Because he favours me.

[*Exit.*]

Mel Gibson – UK – perform Barabas.

[I.i]

Enter BARABAS *in his counting-house, with heaps of gold before him.*

BARABAS. So that of thus much that return was made;
    And of the third part of the Persian ships
    There was the venture summed and satisfied.
    As for those Samnites, and the men of Uz,
    That bought my Spanish oils and wines of Greece,
    Here have I pursed their paltry silverlings.
    Fie, what a trouble 'tis to count this trash!
    Well fare the Arabians who so richly pay
    The things they traffic for with wedge of gold,
    Whereof a man may easily in a day   10
    Tell that which may maintain him all his life.
    The needy groom that never fingered groat,
    Would make a miracle of thus much coin;
    But he whose steel-barred coffers are crammed full,
    And all his life-time hath been tired,
    Wearying his fingers' ends with telling it,
    Would in his age be loath to labour so,
    And for a pound to sweat himself to death.
    Give me the merchants of the Indian mines
    That trade in metal of the purest mould;   20
    The wealthy Moor, that in the eastern rocks
    Without control can pick his riches up,
    And in his house heap pearl like pebble stones,

Globe – Good to see the company take on something more challenging.

Receive them free, and sell them by the weight;
Bags of fiery opals, sapphires, amethysts,
Jacinths, hard topaz, grass-green emeralds,
Beauteous rubies, sparkling diamonds,
And seld-seen costly stones of so great price
As one of them, indifferently rated,
And of a carat of this quantity,   30
May serve in peril of calamity
To ransom great kings from captivity.
This is the ware wherein consists my wealth;
And thus methinks should men of judgement frame
Their means of traffic from the vulgar trade,
And as their wealth increaseth, so enclose
Infinite riches in a little room.
But now how stands the wind?
Into what corner peers my halcyon's bill?
Ha, to the east? Yes. See how stands the vanes?   40
East and by south: why then I hope my ships
I sent for Egypt and the bordering isles
Are gotten up by Nilus' winding banks;
Mine argosy from Alexandria,
Loaden with spice and silks, now under sail,
Are smoothly gliding down by Candy shore
To Malta, through our Mediterranean sea.
But who comes here? How now?

Enter a MERCHANT.

MERCHANT. Barabas, thy ships are safe,
     Riding in Malta road; and all the merchants   50
     With all their merchandise are safe arrived,
     And have sent me to know whether yourself
     Will come and custom them.

BARABAS. The ships are safe thou say'st, and richly fraught?

MERCHANT. They are.

BARABAS.   Why then, go bid them come ashore,
   And bring with them their bills of entry:
   I hope our credit in the custom-house
   Will serve as well as I were present there.
   Go send 'em three-score camels, thirty mules,
   And twenty waggons to bring up the ware.   60
   But art thou master in a ship of mine,
   And is thy credit not enough for that?

MERCHANT. The very custom barely comes to more
   Than many merchants of the town are worth,
   And therefore far exeeeds my credit, Sir.

BARABAS. Go tell 'em the Jew of Malta sent thee, man:
   Tush, who amongst 'em knows not Barabas?

MERCHANT. I go.

BARABAS.   So then, there's somewhat come.
   Sirrah, which of my ships art thou master of?

MERCHANT. Of the Speranza, Sir.

BARABAS.   And saw'st thou not   70
   Mine argosy at Alexandria?
   Thou couldst not come from Egypt, or by Caire,
   But at the entry there into the sea,
   Where Nilus pays his tribute to the main,
   Thou needs must sail by Alexandria.

MERCHANT. I neither saw them nor inquired of them;
   But this we heard some of our seamen say,

They wondered how you durst with so much wealth
Trust such a crazed vessel, and so far.   79

BARABAS. Tush, they are wise. I know her and her strength.
But go, go thou thy ways, discharge thy ship,
And bid my factor bring his loading in.

[*Exit* MERCHANT.]

And yet I wonder at this argosy.

Enter a second MERCHANT.

2 MERCHANT. Thine argosy from Alexandria,
Know, Barabas, doth ride in Malta road,
Laden with riches, and exceeding store
Of Persian silks, of gold, and orient pearl.

BARABAS. How chance you came not with those other ships
That sailed by Egypt?

2 MERCHANT. Sir, we saw 'em not.

BARABAS. Belike they coasted round by Candy shore   90
About their oils or other businesses.
But 'twas ill done of you to come so far
Without the aid or conduct of their ships.

2 MERCHANT. Sir, we were wafted by a Spanish fleet
That never left us till within a league,
That had the galleys of the Turk in chase.

BARABAS. Oh, they were going up to Sicily. Well, go
And bid the merchants and my men dispatch
And come ashore, and see the fraught discharged.

[2] MERCHANT. I go.

Exit.

BARABAS. Thus trolls our fortune in by land and sea, 101
   And thus are we on every side enriched.
   These are the blessings promised to the Jews,
   And herein was old Abram's happiness.
   What more may heaven do for earthly man
   Than thus to pour out plenty in their laps,
   Ripping the bowels of the earth for them,
   Making the sea their servants, and the winds
   To drive their substance with successful blasts?
   Who hateth me but for my happiness? 110
   Or who is honoured now but for his wealth?
   Rather had I, a Jew, be hated thus,
   Than pitied in a Christian poverty;
   For I can see no fruits in all their faith,
   But malice, falsehood, and excessive pride,
   Which methinks fits not their profession.
   Happily some hapless man hath conscience,
   And for his conscience lives in beggary.
   They say we are a scattered nation:
   I cannot tell, but we have scambled up 120
   More wealth by far than those that brag of faith.
   There's Kirriah Jairim, the great Jew of Greece,
   Obed in Bairseth, Nones in Portugal,
   Myself in Malta, some in Italy,
   Many in France, and wealthy every one;
   Ay, wealthier far than any Christian.
   I must confess we come not to be kings:
   That's not our fault: alas, our number's few,
   And crowns come either by succession,
   Or urged by force; and nothing violent, 130
   Oft have I heard tell, can be permanent.
   Give us a peaceful rule; make Christians kings,

That thirst so much for principality.
I have no charge, nor many children,
But one sole daughter, whom I hold as dear
As Agamemnon did his Iphigen;
And all I have is hers. But who comes here?

Enter three JEWS.

1 [JEW]. Tush, tell not me 'twas done of policy.

2 [JEW]. Come therefore, let us go to Barabas,
For he can counsel best in these affairs.   140
And here he comes.

BARABAS.   Why, how now, countrymen?
Why flock you thus to me in multitudes?
What accident's betided to the Jews?

1 [JEW]. A fleet of warlike galleys, Barabas,
Are come from Turkey, and lie in our road:
And they this day sit in the council-house
To entertain them and their embassy.

BARABAS. Why, let 'em come, so they come not to war;
Or let 'em war, so we be conquerors.
(*Aside.*) Nay, let 'em combat, conquer, and kill all,   150
So they spare me, my daughter, and my wealth.

1 [JEW]. Were it for confirmation of a league
They would not come in warlike manner thus.

2 [JEW]. I fear their coming will afflict us all.

BARABAS. Fond men, what dream you of their multitudes?
What need they treat of peace that are in league.
The Turks and those of Malta are in league.
Tut, tut, there is some other matter in't.

1 [JEW]. Why, Barabas, they come for peace or war.

BARABAS. Happily for neither, but to pass along 160
    Towards Venice by the Adriatic sea,
    With whom they have attempted many times,
    But never could effect their stratagem.

3 [JEW]. And very wisely said; it may be so.

2 [JEW]. But there's a meeting in the senate-house,
    And all the Jews in Malta must be there.

BARABAS. Umh; all the Jews in Malta must be there?
    Ay, like enough; why then, let every man
    Provide him, and be there for fashion-sake.
    If anything shall there concern our state, 170
    Assure yourselves I'll look (*Aside*.) unto myself.

1 [JEW]. I know you will. Well, brethren, let us go.

2 [JEW]. Let's take our leaves. Farewell, good Barabas.

BARABAS. Do so. Farewell, Zaareth; farewell, Temainte.

    Exeunt JEWS.

    And Barabas now search this secret out.
    Summon thy senses, call thy wits together:
    These silly men mistake the matter clean.
    Long to the Turk did Malta contribute;
    Which tribute all in policy, I fear,
    The Turks have let increase to such a sum 180
    As all the wealth of Malta cannot pay;
    And now by that advantage thinks, belike,
    To seize upon the town. Ay, that he seeks.
    Howe'er the world go, I'll make sure for one,
    And seek in time to intercept the worst,

Warily guarding that which I ha' got.
Ego mihimet sum semper proximus.
Why, let 'em enter. Let 'em take the town.

[*Exit.*]

*dishonest if i said – un conventional
choice of staging. – Magnificent*

[I.ii]

Enter [FERNEZE *and other*] *Governors of Malta*, KNIGHTS
[OFFICERS *and* READER], *met by* BASHAWS *of the Turk*
[*and*] CALYMATH.

FERNEZE. Now, Bashaws, what demand you at our hands?

BASHAW. Know, Knights of Malta, that we came from
Rhodes,
From Cyprus, Candy, and those other isles
That lie betwixt the Mediterranean seas.

FERNEZE. What's Cyprus, Candy, and those other isles
To us or Malta? What at our hands demand ye?

CALYMATH. The ten years' tribute that remains unpaid.

FERNEZE. Alas, my Lord, the sum is over-great.
I hope your Highness will consider us.   9

CALYMATH. I wish, grave Governors, 'twere in my power
To favour you, but 'tis my father's cause,
Wherein I may not, nay, I dare not dally.

FERNEZE. Then give us leave, great Selim-Calymath.

boy cotted / planned negative review.

CALYMATH. Stand all aside, and let the Knights determine,
  And send to keep our galleys under sail,
  For happily we shall not tarry here.
  Now, Governors, how are you resolved?

FERNEZE. Thus: since your hard conditions are such
  That you will needs have ten years' tribute past,
  We may have time to make collection   20
  Amongst the inhabitants of Malta for't.

BASHAW. That's more than is in our commission.

CALYMATH. What, Callapine, a little courtesy.
  Let's know their time, perhaps it is not long;
  And 'tis more kingly to obtain by peace
  Than to enforce conditions by constraint.
  What respite ask you, Governors?

FERNEZE.   But a month.

CALYMATH. We grant a month, but see you keep your
      promise.
  Now launch our galleys back again to sea,
  Where we'll attend the respite you have ta'en,   30
  And for the money send our messenger.
  Farewell, great Governors and brave Knights of Malta.

  Exeunt [TURKS].

FERNEZE. And all good fortune wait on Calymath.
  Go one and call those Jews of Malta hither:
  Were they not summoned to appear today?

OFFICER. They were, my Lord; and here they come.

  Enter BARABAS *and three* JEWS.

*Sold at, was adapted for it Modern
audience, → Elizabethan characters.*

1 KNIGHT. Have you determined what to say to them?

FERNEZE. Yes, give me leave, and Hebrews now come near.
From the Emperor of Turkey is arrived
Great Selim-Calymath, his highness' son,   40
To levy of us ten years' tribute past,
Now then here know that it concerneth us –

BARABAS. Then, good my Lord, to keep your quiet still,
Your Lordship shall do well to let them have it.

FERNEZE. Soft Barabas, there's more 'longs to't than so.
To what this ten years' tribute will amount,
That we have cast, but cannot compass it
By reason of the wars, that robbed our store;
And therefore are we to request your aid.

BARABAS. Alas, my Lord, we are no soldiers;   50
And what's our aid against so great a Prince?

1 KNIGHT. Tut, Jew, we know thou art no soldier;
Thou art a merchant and a moneyed man,
And 'tis thy money, Barabas, we seek.

BARABAS. How, my Lord, my money?

FERNEZE.   Thine and the rest.
For to be short, amongst you 't must be had.

[1] JEW. Alas, my Lord, the most of us are poor.

FERNEZE. Then let the rich increase your portions.

BARABAS. Are strangers with your tribute to be taxed?   59

2 KNIGHT. Have strangers leave with us to get their wealth?
Then let them with us contribute.

BARABAS. How, equally?

FERNEZE.   No, Jew, like infidels;
    For through our sufferance of your hateful lives
    (Who stand accursed in the sight of Heaven)
    These taxes and afflictions are befallen,
    And therefore thus we are determined.
    Read there the articles of our decrees.

READER. 'First, the tribute-money of the Turks shall all be
    levied amongst the Jews, and each of them to pay one half
    of his estate.'   70

BARABAS. How, half his estate? I hope you mean not mine.

FERNEZE. Read on.

READER. 'Secondly, he that denies to pay, shall straight
    become a Christian.'

BARABAS. How, a Christian? Hum, what's here to do?

READER. 'Lastly, he that denies this, shall absolutely lose all
    he has.'

ALL 3 JEWS. Oh my Lord, we will give half.

BARABAS. Oh earth-metalled villains, and no Hebrews born!
    And will you basely thus submit yourselves   80
    To leave your goods to their arbitrament?

FERNEZE. Why, Barabas, wilt thou be christened?

BARABAS. No, Governor, I will be no convertite.

FERNEZE. Then pay thy half.

BARABAS. Why, know you what you did by this device?
    Half of my substance is a city's wealth.

Governor, it was not got so easily;
Nor will I part so slightly therewithal.

FERNEZE. Sir, half is the penalty of our decree.
Either pay that, or we will seize on all.   90

BARABAS. *Corpo di Dio!* Stay, you shall have half;
Let me be used but as my brethren are.

FERNEZE. No, Jew, thou hast denied the articles,
And now it cannot be recalled.

[*Exeunt* OFFICERS.]

BARABAS. Will you then steal my goods?
Is theft the ground of your religion?

FERNEZE. No, Jew, we take particularly thine
To save the ruin of a multitude:
And better one want for a common good
Than many perish for a private man.   100
Yet, Barabas, we will not banish thee,
But here in Malta, where thou got'st thy wealth,
Live still; and if thou canst, get more.

BARABAS. Christians, what or how can I multiply?
Of naught is nothing made.

1 KNIGHT. From naught at first thou cam'st to little wealth,
From little unto more, from more to most.
If your first curse fall heavy on thy head,
And make thee poor and scorned of all the world,
'Tis not our fault, but thy inherent sin.   110

BARABAS. What? Bring you Scripture to confirm your wrongs?
Preach me not out of my possessions.
Some Jews are wicked, as all Christians are;

But say the tribe that I descended of
Were all in general cast away for sin,
Shall I be tried by their transgression?
The man that dealeth righteously shall live,
And which of you can charge me otherwise?

FERNEZE. Out, wretched Barabas!
  Sham'st thou not thus to justify thyself,   120
  As if we knew not thy profession?
  If thou rely upon thy righteousness,
  Be patient, and thy riches will increase.
  Excess of wealth is cause of covetousness;
  And covetousness, oh 'tis a monstrous sin.

BARABAS. Ay, but theft is worse. Tush, take not from me
      then,
  For that is theft; and if you rob me thus,
  I must be forced to steal, and compass more.

1 KNIGHT. Grave Governors, list not to his exclaims.
  Convert his mansion to a nunnery;   130
  His house will harbour many holy nuns.

FERNEZE. It shall be so.

  Enter OFFICERS.

          Now, officers, have you done?

OFFICER. Ay, my Lord. We have seized upon the goods
  And wares of Barabas, which, being valued,
  Amount to more than all the wealth in Malta;
  And of the other we have seized half.
  Then we'll take order for the residue.

BARABAS. Well then, my Lord, say, are you satisfied?

You have my goods, my money, and my wealth,
My ships, my store, and all that I enjoyed;   140
And having all, you can request no more,
Unless your unrelenting flinty hearts
Suppress all pity in your stony breasts
And now shall move you to bereave my life.

FERNEZE. No, Barabas, to stain our hands with blood
Is far from us and our profession.

BARABAS. Why, I esteem the injury far less,
To take the lives of miserable men
Than be the causers of their misery.
You have my wealth, the labour of my life,   150
The comfort of mine age, my children's hope;
And therefore ne'er distinguish of the wrong.

FERNEZE. Content thee, Barabas, thou hast naught but right.

BARABAS. Your extreme right does me exceeding wrong:
But take it to you i' th' devil's name.

FERNEZE. Come, let us in, and gather of these goods
The money for this tribute of the Turk.

1 KNIGHT. 'Tis necessary that be looked unto;
For if we break our day, we break the league,
And that will prove but simple policy.   160

Exeunt [FERNEZE, KNIGHTS, OFFICERS *and*
READER].

BARABAS. Ay, policy! That's their profession,
And not simplicity, as they suggest.
The plagues of Egypt and the curse of Heaven,
Earth's barrenness and all men's hatred,

Inflict upon them, thou great *Primus Motor.*
And here upon my knees, striking the earth,
I ban their souls to everlasting pains
And extreme tortures of the fiery deep,
That thus have dealt with me in my distress.

1 JEW. Oh yet be patient, gentle Barabas.   170

BARABAS. Oh silly brethren, born to see this day!
    Why stand you thus unmoved with my laments?
    Why weep you not to think upon my wrongs?
    Why pine not I, and die in this distress?

1 JEW. Why, Barabas, as hardly can we brook
    The cruel handling of ourselves in this:
    Thou seest they have taken half our goods.

BARABAS. Why did you yield to their extortion?
    You were a multitude, and I but one;
    And of me only have they taken all.   180

1 JEW. Yet brother Barabas, remember Job.

BARABAS. What tell you me of Job? I wot his wealth
    Was written thus: he had seven thousand sheep,
    Three thousand camels, and two hundred yoke
    Of labouring oxen, and five hundred
    She-asses; but for every one of those,
    Had they been valued at indifferent rate,
    I had at home, and in mine argosy,
    And other ships that came from Egypt last,
    As much as would have bought his beasts and him,   190
    And yet have kept enough to live upon;
    So that not he but I may curse the day,
    Thy fatal birthday, forlorn Barabas;

And henceforth wish for an eternal night,
That clouds of darkness may enclose my flesh,
And hide these extreme sorrows from mine eyes:
For only I have toiled to inherit here
The months of vanity and loss of time,
And painful nights have been appointed me.

2 JEW. Good Barabas, be patient.   200

BARABAS. Ay, ay, pray leave me in my patience.
You, that were ne'er possessed of wealth, are pleased with want.
But give him liberty at least to mourn,
That in a field amidst his enemies
Doth see his soldiers slain, himself disarmed,
And knows no means of his recovery.
Ay, let me sorrow for this sudden chance;
'Tis in the trouble of my spirit I speak:
Great injuries are not so soon forgot.

1 JEW. Come, let us leave him in his ireful mood,   210
Our words will but increase his ecstasy.

2 JEW. On then: but trust me, 'tis a misery
To see a man in such affliction.
Farewell Barabas.

Exeunt.

BARABAS.   Ay, fare you well.
See the simplicity of these base slaves,
Who, for the villains have no wit themselves,
Think me to be a senseless lump of clay,
That will with every water wash to dirt.
No, Barabas is born to better chance,

And framed of finer mould than common men,   220
That measure naught but by the present time.
A reaching thought will search his deepest wits,
And cast with cunning for the time to come;
For evils are apt to happen every day.
But whither wends my beauteous Abigail?

Enter ABIGAIL, *the Jew's daughter.*

Oh, what has made my lovely daughter sad?
What, woman, moan not for a little loss;
Thy father has enough in store for thee.

ABIGAIL. Not for myself, but aged Barabas,
    Father, for thee lamenteth Abigail.   230
    But I will learn to leave these fruitless tears,
    And urged thereto with my afflictions,
    With fierce exclaims run to the senate-house,
    And in the senate reprehend them all,
    And rent their hearts with tearing of my hair,
    Till they reduce the wrongs done to my father.

BARABAS. No, Abigail, things past recovery
    Are hardly cured with exclamations.
    Be silent, Daughter; sufferance breeds ease,
    And time may yield us an occasion,   240
    Which on the sudden cannot serve the turn.
    Besides, my girl, think me not all so fond
    As negligently to forgo so much
    Without provision for thyself and me.
    Ten thousand portagues, besides great pearls,
    Rich costly jewels, and stones infinite,
    Fearing the worst of this before it fell,
    I closely hid.

ABIGAIL. Where, Father?

BARABAS.   In my house, my girl.

ABIGAIL. Then shall they ne'er be seen of Barabas;
For they have seized upon thy house and wares.   250

BARABAS. But they will give me leave once more, I trow,
To go into my house.

ABIGAIL.   That may they not,
For there I left the Governor placing nuns,
Displacing me; and of thy house they mean
To make a nunnery, where none but their own sect
Must enter in, men generally barred.

BARABAS. My gold, my gold, and all my wealth is gone.
You partial heavens, have I deserved this plague?
What, will you thus oppose me, luckless stars,
To make me desperate in my poverty?   260
And knowing me impatient in distress,
Think me so mad as I will hang myself,
That I may vanish o'er the earth in air,
And leave no memory that e'er I was.
No, I will live, nor loathe I this my life:
And since you leave me in the ocean thus
To sink or swim, and put me to my shifts,
I'll rouse my senses, and awake myself.
Daughter, I have it: thou perceiv'st the plight
Wherein these Christians have oppressed me: 270
Be ruled by me, for in extremity
We ought to make bar of no policy.

ABIGAIL. Father, whate'er it be, to injure them
That have so manifestly wronged us,

What will not Abigail attempt?   → Jewishness

Gibson → renamed Catholic.

BARABAS.   Why, so;
Then thus: thou told'st me they have turned my house
Into a nunnery, and some nuns are there.

ABIGAIL. I did.

BARABAS.   Then, Abigail, there must my girl
Entreat the Abbess to be entertained.

ABIGAIL. How, as a nun?

Religious hypocrasy

BARABAS. Ay, Daughter; for religion   280
Hides many mischiefs from suspicion.

ABIGAIL. Ay, but Father they will suspect me there.

BARABAS. Let em suspect, but be thou so precise
As they may think it done of holiness.
Entreat 'em fair, and give them friendly speech,
And seem to them as if thy sins were great,
Till thou hast gotten to be entertained.

ABIGAIL. Thus, Father, shall I much dissemble.

BARABAS.   Tush,
As good dissemble that thou never mean'st
As first mean truth, and then dissemble it: 290
A counterfeit profession is better
Than unseen hypocrisy.

ABIGAIL. Well, Father, say I be entertained,
What then shall follow?

BARABAS.   This shall follow then:
There have I hid, close underneath the plank
That runs along the upper-chamber floor,

Baraban vs pragmatic.

Director – neatly &
Cleverly readapted. – Jewish

The gold and jewels which I kept for thee.
But here they come; be cunning, Abigail.

ABIGAIL. Then, Father, go with me.

BARABAS. No, Abigail, in this   300
    It is not necessary I be seen;
    For I will seem offended with thee for't.
    Be close, my girl, for this must fetch my gold.

Enter three FRIARS [*including* JACOMO, BARNARDINE]
and two NUNS [*one an* ABBESS].

JACOMO. Sisters, we now are almost at the new-made
        nunnery.

ABBESS. The better; for we love not to be seen.
    'Tis thirty winters long since some of us
    Did stray so far amongst the multitude.

JACOMO. But, Madam, this house
    And waters of this new-made nunnery   310
    Will much delight you.

ABBESS. It may be so. But who comes here?

ABIGAIL. Grave Abbess, and you happy virgins' guide,
    Pity the state of a distressed maid.

ABBESS. What art thou, Daughter?

ABIGAIL. The hopeless daughter of a hapless Jew,
    The Jew of Malta, wretched Barabas,
    Sometimes the owner of a goodly house,
    Which they have now turned to a nunnery.

ABBESS. Well, Daughter, say, what is thy suit with us?   320

Tragedy of piece → Thomas hyd
- Spanish Tragedy...
    gruesome ending.

ABIGAIL. Fearing the afflictions which my father feels
    Proceed from sin or want of faith in us,
    I'd pass away my life in penitence
    And be a novice in your nunnery,
    To make atonement for my labouring soul.

JACOMO. No doubt, Brother, but this proceedeth of the spirit.

BARNARDINE. Ay, and of a moving spirit too, Brother: but
        come,
    Let us entreat she may be entertained.

ABBESS. Well, Daughter, we admit you for a nun.

ABIGAIL. First let me as a novice learn to frame   330
    My solitary life to your strait laws,
    And let me lodge where I was wont to lie.
    I do not doubt, by your divine precepts
    And mine own industry, but to profit much.

BARABAS (aside). As much, I hope, as all I hid is worth.

ABBESS. Come Daughter, follow us.

BARABAS.   Why how now Abigail,
    What mak'st thou amongst these hateful Christians?

JACOMO. Hinder her not, thou man of little faith,
    For she has mortified herself.

BARABAS.   How, mortified?

JACOMO. And is admitted to the sisterhood.   340

BARABAS. Child of perdition, and thy father's shame,
    What wilt thou do among these hateful fiends?
    I charge thee on my blessing that thou leave
    These devils and their damned heresy.

ABIGAIL. Father, give me –

BARABAS.　　　　　　　　Nay, back, Abigail –

Whispers to her.

And think upon the jewels and the gold;
The board is marked thus that covers it.
Away, accursed, from thy father's sight!

JACOMO. Barabas, although thou art in misbelief,
And wilt not see thine own afflictions,　　　　　　350
Yet let thy daughter be no longer blind.

BARABAS. Blind, Friar, I reck not thy persuasions.
[*Aside to her.*] The board is marked thus † that covers it.
For I had rather die than see her thus.
Wilt thou forsake me too in my distress,
Seduced Daughter? (*Aside to her.*) Go, forget not –
Becomes it Jews to be so credulous?
(*Aside to her.*) Tomorrow early I'll be at the door –
No, come not at me; if thou wilt be damned,
Forget me, see me not, and so be gone.　　　　　　360
(*Aside.*) Farewell, remember tomorrow morning.
Out, out, thou wretch.

[*Exeunt separately.*] *Enter* MATHIAS.

MATHIAS. Who's this? Fair Abigail, the rich Jew's daughter
Become a nun? Her father's sudden fall
Has humbled her and brought her down to this.
Tut, she were fitter for a tale of love
Than to be tired out with orisons;
And better would she far become a bed
Embraced in a friendly lover's arms,
Than rise at midnight to a solemn mass.　　　　　　370

Enter LODOWICK.

LODOWICK. Why, how now, Don Mathias, in a dump?

MATHIAS. Believe me, noble Lodowick, I have seen
  The strangest sight, in my opinion,
  That ever I beheld.

LODOWICK.   What was't, I prithee?

MATHIAS. A fair young maid, scarce fourteen years of age,
  The sweetest flower in Cytherea's field,
  Cropped from the pleasures of the fruitful earth,
  And strangely metamorphosed [to a] nun.

LODOWICK. But say, what was she?

MATHIAS.   Why, the rich Jew's daughter.
LODOWICK. What Barabas, whose goods were lately seized?
  Is she so fair?   380

MATHIAS.   And matchless beautiful;
  As had you seen her, 'twould have moved your heart,
  Though countermured with walls of brass, to love,
  Or at the least, to pity.

LODOWICK. And if she be so fair as you report,
  'Twere time well spent to go and visit her.
  How say you, shall we?

MATHIAS. I must and will, Sir, there's no remedy.

LODOWICK. And so will I too, or it shall go hard.
  Farewell, Mathias.

MATHIAS.   Farewell, Lodowick.

  Exeunt.

[II.i]

Enter BARABAS *with a light.*

BARABAS. Thus like the sad presaging raven that tolls
    The sick man's passport in her hollow beak,
    And in the shadow of the silent night
    Doth shake contagion from her sable wings,
    Vexed and tormented runs poor Barabas
    With fatal curses towards these Christians.
    The incertain pleasures of swift-footed time
    Have ta'en their flight, and left me in despair;
    And of my former riches rests no more
    But bare remembrance, like a soldier's scar,   10
    That has no further comfort for his maim.
    Oh thou, that with a fiery pillar led'st
    The sons of Israel through the dismal shades,
    Light Abraham's offspring, and direct the hand
    Of Abigail this night; or let the day
    Turn to eternal darkness after this.
    No sleep can fasten on my watchful eyes,
    Nor quiet enter my distempered thoughts,
    Till I have answer of my Abigail.

Enter ABIGAIL *above.*

ABIGAIL. Now have I happily espied a time   20
    To search the plank my father did appoint;
    And here behold (unseen) where I have found
    The gold, the pearls, and jewels, which he hid.

BARABAS. Now I remember those old women's words
 Who in my wealth would tell me winter's tales
 And speak of spirits and ghosts that glide by night
 About the place where treasure hath been hid.
 And now methinks that I am one of those;
 For whilst I live, here lives my soul's sole hope,
 And when I die, here shall my spirit walk.   30

ABIGAIL. Now that my father's fortune were so good
 As but to be about this happy place.
 'Tis not so happy: yet, when we parted last,
 He said he would attend me in the morn.
 Then, gentle Sleep, where'er his body rests,
 Give charge to Morpheus that he may dream
 A golden dream, and of the sudden wake,
 Come and receive the treasure I have found.

BARABAS. *Bien para todos mi ganada no es;*
 As good go on as sit so sadly thus.   40
 But stay, what star shines yonder in the east?
 The loadstar of my life, if Abigail.
 Who's there?

ABIGAIL. Who's that?

BARABAS.   Peace, Abigail, 'tis I.

ABIGAIL. Then, Father, here receive thy happiness.

BARABAS. Hast thou't?

ABIGAIL.   Here. (*Throws down bags.*) Hast thou't?
 There's more, and more, and more.

BARABAS.   Oh my girl,
 My gold, my fortune, my felicity,

Strength to my soul, death to mine enemy.
Welcome the first beginner of my bliss.
Oh Abigail, Abigail, that I had thee here too,   50
Then my desires were fully satisfied:
But I will practise thy enlargement thence.
Oh girl, oh gold, oh beauty, oh my bliss!

Hugs his bags.

ABIGAIL. Father, it draweth towards midnight now,
    And 'bout this time the nuns begin to wake.
    To shun suspicion, therefore, let us part.

BARABAS. Farewell my joy, and by my fingers take
    A kiss from him that sends it from his soul.
    Now Phoebus ope the eyelids of the day,
    And for the raven wake the morning lark,   60
    That I may hover with her in the air,
    Singing o'er these as she does o'er her young:
    Hermoso placer de los dineros.

Exeunt.

[II.ii]

Enter [FERNEZE, the] Governor, Martin del BOSCO, the
KNIGHTS [*and* OFFICERS].

FERNEZE. Now, Captain, tell us whither thou art bound?
    Whence is thy ship that anchors in our road?
    And why thou cam'st ashore without our leave?

BOSCO. Governor of Malta, hither am I bound;
    My ship, the Flying Dragon, is of Spain,
    And so am I, del Bosco is my name,
    Vice-Admiral unto the Catholic King.

1 KNIGHT. 'Tis true, my Lord, therefore entreat him well.

BOSCO. Our fraught is Grecians, Turks, and Afric Moors;
    For late upon the coast of Corsica,   10
    Because we vailed not to the Turkish fleet,
    Their creeping galleys had us in the chase;
    But suddenly the wind began to rise,
    And then we luffed and tacked, and fought at ease.
    Some have we fired, and many have we sunk;
    But one amongst the rest became our prize:
    The captain's slain; the rest remain our slaves,
    Of whom we would make sale in Malta here.

FERNEZE. Martin del Bosco, I have heard of thee.
    Welcome to Malta, and to all of us;   20
    But to admit a sale of these thy Turks,
    We may not, nay we dare not give consent,
    By reason of a tributary league.

1 KNIGHT. Del Bosco, as thou lovest and honour'st us,
    Persuade our Governor against the Turk.
    This truce we have is but in hope of gold,
    And with that sum he craves might we wage war.

BOSCO. Will Knights of Malta be in league with Turks,
    And buy it basely too for sums of gold?
    My Lord, remember that, to Europe's shame,   30
    The Christian Isle of Rhodes, from whence you came,
    Was lately lost, and you were stated here

To be at deadly enmity with Turks.

FERNEZE. Captain, we know it, but our force is small.

BOSCO. What is the sum that Calymath requires?

FERNEZE. A hundred thousand crowns.

BOSCO. My Lord and King hath title to this isle,
    And he means quickly to expel you hence.
    Therefore be ruled by me, and keep the gold:
    I'll write unto his Majesty for aid,   40
    And not depart until I see you free.

FERNEZE. On this condition shall thy Turks be sold.
    Go, officers, and set them straight in show.

    [*Exeunt* OFFICERS.]

    Bosco, thou shalt be Malta's General;
    We and our warlike Knights will follow thee
    Against these barbarous misbelieving Turks.

BOSCO. So shall you imitate those you succeed;
    For when their hideous force environed Rhodes,
    Small though the number was that kept the town,
    They fought it out, and not a man survived   50
    To bring the hapless news to Christendom.

FERNEZE. So will we fight it out. Come, let s away.
    Proud-daring Calymath, instead of gold,
    We'll send thee bullets wrapped in smoke and fire.
    Claim tribute where thou wilt, we are resolved:
    Honour is bought with blood, and not with gold.

    Exeunt.

[II.iii]

Enter OFFICERS *with* SLAVES.

1 OFFICER. This is the market-place, here let 'em stand:
    Fear not their sale, for they'll be quickly bought.

2 OFFICER. Every one's price is written on his back,
    And so much must they yield, or not be sold.

1 OFFICER. Here comes the Jew; had not his goods been
        seized,
    He'd give us present money for them all.

    Enter BARABAS.

BARABAS. In spite of these swine-eating Christians
    (Unchosen nation, never circumcised,
    Such as, poor villains, were ne'er thought upon
    Till Titus and Vespasian conquered us),   10
    Am I become as wealthy as I was.
    They hoped my daughter would ha' been a nun;
    But she's at home, and I have bought a house
    As great and fair as is the Governor's;
    And there in spite of Malta will I dwell,
    Having Ferneze's hand, whose heart I'll have;
    Ay, and his son's too, or it shall go hard.
    I am not of the tribe of Levi, I,
    That can so soon forget an injury.
    We Jews can fawn like spaniels when we please,   20
    And when we grin we bite, yet are our looks
    As innocent and harmless as a lamb's.
    I learned in Florence how to kiss my hand,
    Heave up my shoulders when they call me dog,
    And duck as low as any bare-foot friar,

Hoping to see them starve upon a stall,
Or else be gathered for in our synagogue,
That, when the offering-basin comes to me,
Even for charity I may spit into't.
Here comes Don Lodowick, the Governor's son,   30
One that I love for his good father's sake.

Enter LODOWICK.

LODOWICK. I hear the wealthy Jew walked this way;
I'll seek him out, and so insinuate
That I may have a sight of Abigail,
For Don Mathias tells me she is fair.

BARABAS. Now will I show myself to have more of the
serpent than the dove; that is, more knave than fool.

LODOWICK. Yond walks the Jew, now for fair Abigail.

BARABAS. Ay, ay, no doubt but she's at your command.   39

LODOWICK. Barabas, thou know'st I am the Governor's son.

BARABAS. I would you were his father too, Sir; that's all the
harm I wish you. [*Aside*.] The slave looks like a hog's cheek
new singed.

LODOWICK. Whither walk'st thou, Barabas?

BARABAS. No further. 'Tis a custom held with us,
That when we speak with Gentiles like to you,
We turn into the air to purge ourselves:
For unto us the promise doth belong.

LODOWICK. Well, Barabas, canst help me to a diamond?

BARABAS. Oh, Sir, your father had my diamonds.   50
Yet I have one left that will serve your turn –

(*Aside.*) I mean my daughter; but ere he shall have her
    I'll sacrifice her on a pile of wood:
    I ha' the poison of the city for him,
    And the white leprosy.

LODOWICK. What sparkle does it give without a foil?

BARABAS. The diamond that I talk of ne'er was foiled –
    [*Aside.*] But when he touches it it will be foiled –
    Lord Lodowick, it sparkles bright and fair.

LODOWICK. Is it square or pointed, pray let me know?   60

BARABAS. Pointed it is, good Sir, (*Aside.*) but not for you.

LODOWICK. I like it much the better.

BARABAS.   So do I too.

LODOWICK. How shows it by night?

BARABAS.   Outshines Cynthia's rays:
    (*Aside.*) You'll like it better far a-nights than days.

LODOWICK. And what's the price?

BARABAS [*Aside*].   Your life, and if you have it.
    Oh my Lord,
    We will not jar about the price: come to my house,
    And I will give't your honour (*Aside.*) with a vengeance.

LODOWICK. No, Barabas, I will deserve it first.

BARABAS. Good Sir,   70
    Your father has deserved it at my hands,
    Who of mere charity and Christian ruth,
    To bring me to religious purity,
    And as it were in catechizing sort,

To make me mindful of my mortal sins,
Against my will, and whether I would or no,
Seized all I had, and thrust me out-a-doors,
And made my house a place for nuns most chaste.

LODOWICK. No doubt your soul shall reap the fruit of it.

BARABAS. Ay, but my Lord, the harvest is far off.   80
And yet I know the prayers of those nuns
And holy friars, having money for their pains,
Are wondrous; (*Aside.*) and indeed do no man good;
And, seeing they are not idle, but still doing,
'Tis likely they in time may reap some fruit,
I mean, in fullness of perfection.

LODOWICK. Good Barabas, glance not at our holy nuns.

BARABAS. No, but I do it through a burning zeal –
(*Aside.*) Hoping ere long to set the house a-fire;
For, though they do a while increase and multiply,   90
I'll have a saying to that nunnery –
As for the diamond, Sir, I told you of,
Come home, and there's no price shall make us part,
Even for your honourable father's sake –
(*Aside.*) It shall go hard but I will see your death –
But now I must be gone to buy a slave.

LODOWICK. And, Barabas, I'll bear thee company.

BARABAS. Come then; here's the market-place. What's the
price of this slave? Two hundred crowns? Do the Turks
weigh so much?   100

[1] OFFICER. Sir, that's his price.

BARABAS. What, can he steal, that you demand so much?

Belike he has some new trick for a purse;
And if he has, he is worth three hundred plats,
So that, being bought, the town seal might be got
To keep him for his lifetime from the gallows.
The sessions-day is critical to thieves,
And few or none 'scape but by being purged.

LODOWICK. Ratest thou this Moor but at two hundred plats?

1 OFFICER. No more, my Lord.   110

BARABAS. Why should this Turk be dearer than that Moor?

[1] OFFICER. Because he is young and has more qualities.

BARABAS. What, hast the philosopher's stone? And thou
     hast, break my head with it, I'll forgive thee.

SLAVE. No Sir; I can cut and shave.

BARABAS. Let me see, Sirrah, are you not an old shaver?

SLAVE. Alas, Sir, I am a very youth.

BARABAS. A youth? I'll buy you, and marry you to Lady
     Vanity, if you do well.

SLAVE. I will serve you, Sir.   120

BARABAS. Some wicked trick or other. It may be, under
     colour of shaving, thou'lt cut my throat for my goods. Tell
     me, hast thou thy health well?

SLAVE. Ay, passing well.

BARABAS. So much the worse; I must have one that's sickly,
     and be but for sparing victuals. 'Tis not a stone of beef a
     day will maintain you in these chops; let me see one that's
     somewhat leaner.

1 OFFICER. Here's a leaner; how like you him?

BARABAS. Where was thou born?   130

ITHAMORE. In Thrace; brought up in Arabia.

BARABAS. So much the better, thou art for my turn.
　　An hundred crowns? I'll have him; there's the coin.

1 OFFICER. Then mark him, Sir, and take him hence.

BARABAS. Ay, mark him, you were best; for this is he
　　That by my help shall do much villainy.
　　My Lord, farewell. Come, Sirrah, you are mine.
　　As for the diamond, it shall be yours;
　　I pray, Sir, be no stranger at my house,
　　All that I have shall be at your command.   140

　　Enter MATHIAS [*and* KATHARINE, *his*] *Mother.*

MATHIAS. What makes the Jew and Lodowick so private?
　　I fear me 'tis about fair Abigail.

BARABAS. Yonder comes Don Mathias, let us stay:
　　He loves my daughter, and she holds him dear;
　　But I have sworn to frustrate both their hopes,
　　And be revenged upon the Governor.

　　[*Exit* LODOWICK.]

KATHARINE. This Moor is comeliest, is he not? Speak, Son.

MATHIAS. No, this is the better, Mother, view this well.

BARABAS. Seem not to know me here before your mother,
　　Lest she mistrust the match that is in hand.   150
　　When you have brought her home, come to my house;
　　Think of me as thy father. Son, farewell.

MATHIAS. But wherefore talked Don Lodowick with you?

BARABAS. Tush, man, we talked of diamonds, not of Abigail.

KATHARINE. Tell me, Mathias, is not that the Jew?

BARABAS. As for the comment on the Maccabees,
I have it, Sir, and 'tis at your command.

MATHIAS. Yes, Madam, and my talk with him was
About the borrowing of a book or two.   159

KATHARINE. Converse not with him; he is cast off from
heaven.
Thou hast thy crowns, Fellow. Come, let's away.

MATHIAS. Sirrah, Jew, remember the book.

BARABAS. Marry will I, Sir.

Exeunt [KATHARINE *and* MATHIAS, *with a* SLAVE].

[1] OFFICER. Come, I have made a reasonable market; let's
away.

[*Exeunt* OFFICERS *with* SLAVES.]

BARABAS. Now let me know thy name, and therewithal
Thy birth, condition, and profession.

ITHAMORE. Faith, Sir, my birth is but mean, my name's
Ithamore, my profession what you please.

BARABAS. Hast thou no trade? Then listen to my words,
And I will teach [thee] that shall stick by thee.   170
First be thou void of these affections:
Compassion, love, vain hope, and heartless fear;
Be moved at nothing, see thou pity none,
But to thyself smile when the Christians moan.

ITHAMORE. Oh, brave, Master, I worship your nose for this.

BARABAS. As for myself, I walk abroad a-nights,
    And kill sick people groaning under walls;
    Sometimes I go about and poison wells;
    And now and then, to cherish Christian thieves,
    I am content to lose some of my crowns,   180
    That I may, walking in my gallery,
    See 'em go pinioned along by my door.
    Being young, I studied physic, and began
    To practise first upon the Italian;
    There I enriched the priests with burials,
    And always kept the sexton's arms in ure
    With digging graves and ringing dead men's knells.
    And after that, was I an engineer,
    And in the wars 'twixt France and Germany,
    Under pretence of helping Charles the Fifth,   190
    Slew friend and enemy with my stratagems.
    Then after that was I an usurer,
    And with extorting, cozening, forfeiting,
    And tricks belonging unto brokery,
    I filled the gaols with bankrouts in a year,
    And with young orphans planted hospitals,
    And every moon made some or other mad,
    And now and then one hang himself for grief,
    Pinning upon his breast a long great scroll
    How I with interest tormented him.   200
    But mark how I am blest for plaguing them:
    I have as much coin as will buy the town.
    But tell me now, how hast thou spent thy time?

ITHAMORE. Faith, Master,
    In setting Christian villages on fire,

Chaining of eunuchs, binding galley-slaves.
One time I was an hostler in an inn,
And in the night-time secretly would I steal
To travellers' chambers, and there cut their throats;
Once at Jerusalem, where the pilgrims kneeled,   210
I strowed powder on the marble stones,
And therewithal their knees would rankle so
That I have laughed a-good to see the cripples
Go limping home to Christendom on stilts.

BARABAS. Why, this is something: make account of me
As of thy fellow; we are villains both:
Both circumcised, we hate Christians both.
Be true and secret, thou shalt want no gold.
But stand aside, here comes Don Lodowick.

Enter LODOWICK.

LODOWICK. Oh Barabas, well met.   220
Where is the diamond you told me of?

BARABAS. I have it for you, Sir: please you walk in with me –
What ho, Abigail; open the door I say.

Enter ABIGAIL.

ABIGAIL. In good time, father, here are letters come
From Ormus, and the post stays here within.

BARABAS. Give me the letters; Daughter, do you hear?
Entertain Lodowick, the Governor's son,
With all the courtesy you can afford,
Provided that you keep your maidenhead.
Use him as if he were a (*Aside.*) Philistine;   230
Dissemble, swear, protest, vow to love him:
He is not of the seed of Abraham.

I am a little busy, Sir; pray pardon me.
Abigail, bid him welcome for my sake.

ABIGAIL. For your sake and his own he's welcome hither.

BARABAS. Daughter, a word more: kiss him, speak him fair,
And like a cunning Jew so cast about
That ye be both made sure ere you come out.

ABIGAIL. Oh father, Don Mathias is my love.

BARABAS. I know it: yet I say make love to him;   240
Do, it is requisite it should be so.
Nay on my life, it is my factor's hand;
But go you in, I'll think upon the account.

[*Exeunt* ABIGAIL *and* LODOWICK.]

The account is made, for Lodowick dies.
My factor sends me word a merchant's fled
That owes me for a hundred tun of wine:
I weigh it thus much; I have wealth enough;
For now by this has he kissed Abigail,
And she vows love to him, and he to her.
And sure as Heaven rained manna for the Jews,   250
So sure shall he and Don Mathias die:
His father was my chiefest enemy.

Enter MATHIAS.

Whither goes Don Mathias? Stay a while.

MATHIAS. Whither but to my fair love Abigail?

BARABAS. Thou know'st, and heaven can witness it is true,
That I intend my daughter shall be thine.

MATHIAS. Ay, Barabas, or else thou wrong'st me much.

BARABAS. Oh heaven forbid I should have such a thought!
    Pardon me though I weep: the Governor's son
    Will, whether I will or no, have Abigail;   260
    He sends her letters, bracelets, jewels, rings.

MATHIAS. Does she receive them?

BARABAS. She? No, Mathias, no, but sends them back,
    And when he comes, she locks herself up fast;
    Yet through the key-hole will he talk to her,
    While she runs to the window looking out
    When you should come and hale him from the door.

MATHIAS. Oh treacherous Lodowick!

BARABAS. Even now, as I came home, he slipped me in,
    And I am sure he is with Abigail.   270

MATHIAS. I'll rouse him thence.

BARABAS. Not for all Malta; therefore sheathe your sword.
    If you love me, no quarrels in my house;
    But steal you in, and seem to see him not:
    I'll give him such a warning ere he goes
    As he shall have small hopes of Abigail.
    Away, for here they come.

    Enter LODOWICK, ABIGAIL.

MATHIAS. What hand in hand? I cannot suffer this.

BARABAS. Mathias, as thou lov'st me, not a word.   279

MATHIAS. Well, let it pass. Another time shall serve.

    Exit.

LODOWICK. Barabas, is not that the widow's son?

BARABAS. Ay, and take heed, for he hath sworn your death.

LODOWICK. My death? What, is the base-born peasant mad?

BARABAS. No, no; but happily he stands in fear
Of that which you, I think, ne'er dream upon,
My daughter here, a paltry silly girl.

LODOWICK. Why, loves she Don Mathias?

BARABAS. Doth she not with her smiling answer you?

ABIGAIL [*aside*]. He has my heart, I smile against my will.

LODOWICK. Barabas, thou know'st I have loved thy
daughter long.   290

BARABAS. And so has she done you, even from a child.

LODOWICK. And now I can no longer hold my mind.

BARABAS. Nor I the affection that I bear to you.

LODOWICK. This is thy diamond. Tell me, shall I have it?

BARABAS. Win it, and wear it; it is yet unfoiled.
Oh but I know your Lordship would disdain
To marry with the daughter of a Jew:
And yet I'll give her many a golden cross,
With Christian posies round about the ring.

LODOWICK. 'Tis not thy wealth, but her that I esteem;   300
Yet crave I thy consent.

BARABAS. And mine you have; yet let me talk to her.
(*Aside.*) This offspring of Cain, this Jebusite
That never tasted of the Passover
Nor e'er shall see the land of Canaan
Nor our Messias that is yet to come,

This gentle maggot, Lodowick I mean,
Must be deluded: let him have thy hand,
But keep thy heart till Don Mathias comes.

ABIGAIL. What, shall I be betrothed to Lodowick?   310

BARABAS. It's no sin to deceive a Christian;
For they themselves hold it a principle,
Faith is not to be held with heretics:
But all are heretics that are not Jews.
This follows well, and therefore, daughter, fear not.
I have entreated her, and she will grant.

LODOWICK. Then gentle Abigail, plight thy faith to me.

ABIGAIL. I cannot choose, seeing my father bids:
Nothing but death shall part my love and me.   319

LODOWICK. Now have I that for which my soul hath longed.

BARABAS (*aside*). So have not I; but yet I hope I shall.

ABIGAIL. Oh wretched Abigail, what hast thee done?

LODOWICK. Why on the sudden is your colour changed?

ABIGAIL. I know not, but farewell, I must be gone.

BARABAS. Stay her, but let her not speak one word more.

LODOWICK. Mute o' the sudden; here's a sudden change.

BARABAS. Oh muse not at it; 'tis the Hebrews' guise
That maidens new-betrothed should weep a while.
Trouble her not, sweet Lodowick, depart;
She is thy wife, and thou shalt be mine heir.   330

LODOWICK. Oh, is't the custom? Then I am resolved:
But rather let the brightsome heavens be dim,

And nature's beauty choke with stifling clouds,
Than my fair Abigail should frown on me.
There comes the villain; now I'll be revenged.

Enter MATHIAS.

BARABAS. Be quiet, Lodowick; it is enough
    That I have made thee sure to Abigail.

LODOWICK. Well, let him go.

Exit.

BARABAS. Well, but for me, as you went in at doors
    You had been stabbed, but not a word on't now.   340
    Here must no speeches pass, nor swords be drawn.

MATHIAS. Suffer me, Barabas, but to follow him.

BARABAS. No; so shall I, if any hurt be done,
    Be made an accessary of your deeds.
    Revenge it on him when you meet him next.

MATHIAS. For this I'll have his heart.

BARABAS. Do so; lo, here I give thee Abigail.

MATHIAS. What greater gift can poor Mathias have?
    Shall Lodowick rob me of so fair a love?
    My life is not so dear as Abigail.   350

BARABAS. My heart misgives me that to cross your love
    He's with your mother; therefore after him.

MATHIAS. What, is he gone unto my mother?

BARABAS. Nay, if you will, stay till she comes herself.

MATHIAS. I cannot stay; for, if my mother come,
    She'll die with grief.

Exit.

ABIGAIL. I cannot take my leave of him for tears.
　　Father, why have you thus incensed them both?

BARABAS. What's that to thee?

ABIGAIL. 　　　　　　　I'll make 'em friends again.

BARABAS. You'll make 'em friends? Are there not Jews enow
　　　　in Malta, 　　　　　　　　　　　　　　　　360
But thou must dote upon a Christian?

ABIGAIL. I will have Don Mathias; he is my love.

BARABAS. Yes, you shall have him. Go, put her in.

ITHAMORE. Ay, I'll put her in.

　　[*Puts* ABIGAIL *in.*]

BARABAS. Now tell me, Ithamore, how lik'st thou this?

ITHAMORE. Faith, Master, I think by this
　　You purchase both their lives: is it not so?

BARABAS. True, and it shall be cunningly performed.

ITHAMORE. Oh, Master, that I might have a hand in this.

BARABAS. Ay, so thou shalt, 'tis thou must do the deed. 370
Take this, and bear it to Mathias straight,
　　And tell him that it comes from Lodowick.

ITHAMORE. 'Tis poisoned, is it not?

BARABAS. No, no; and yet it might be done that way.
　　It is a challenge feigned from Lodowick,

ITHAMORE. Fear not, I'll so set his heart afire,
　　That he shall verily think it comes from him.

BARABAS. I cannot choose but like thy readiness;
   Yet be not rash, but do it cunningly.   379

ITHAMORE. As I behave myself in this, employ me
   hereafter.

BARABAS. Away, then.

   Exit [ITHAMORE].

   So, now will I go in to Lodowick,
   And like a cunning spirit feign some lie,
   Till I have set 'em both at enmity.

   Exit.

[III.i]

Enter [BELLAMIRA] *a courtesan.*

BELLAMIRA. Since this town was besieged, my gain
    grows cold:
  The time has been, that but for one bare night
  A hundred ducats have been freely given;
  But now against my will I must be chaste;
  And yet I know my beauty doth not fail.
  From Venice merchants, and from Padua
  Were wont to come rare-witted gentlemen,
  Scholars I mean, learned and liberal;
  And now, save Pilia-Borza, comes there none,
  And he is very seldom from my house;   10
  And here he comes.

Enter PILIA-BORZA.

PILIA-BORZA. Hold thee, wench, there's something for thee
to spend.

BELLAMIRA. 'Tis silver; I disdain it.

PILIA-BORZA. Ay, but the Jew has gold,
  And I will have it, or it shall go hard.

BELLAMIRA. Tell me, how cam'st thou by this?

PILIA-BORZA. Faith, walking the back lanes through the
gardens, I chanced to cast mine eye up to the Jew's

counting-house, where I saw some bags of money, and
in the night I clambered up with my hooks; and as I was
taking my choice, I heard a rumbling in the house; so I
took only this, and run my way. But here's the Jew's man.

Enter ITHAMORE.

BELLAMIRA. Hide the bag.   23

PILIA-BORZA. Look not towards him, let's away. Zoons,
what a looking thou keep'st, thou'lt betray 's anon.

[*Exeunt* BELLAMIRA *and* PILIA-BORZA.]

ITHAMORE. Oh the sweetest face that ever I beheld! I
know she is a courtesan by her attire: now would I give a
hundred of the Jew's crowns that I had such a concubine.
Well, I have delivered the challenge in such sort,
As meet they will, and fighting die; brave sport.

Exit.

[III, ii]

Enter MATHIAS.

MATHIAS. This is the place, now Abigail shall see
    Whether Mathias holds her dear or no.

Enter LODOWICK *reading.*

What, dares the villain write in such base terms?

LODOWICK. I did it; and revenge it if thou dar'st.

Fight. Enter BARABAS *above.*

BARABAS. Oh bravely fought! and yet they thrust not home.
 Now Lodovico, now Mathias; so! [*Both fall.*]
 So now they have showed themselves to be tall fellows.

[VOICES] *within.* Part 'em, part 'em.

BARABAS. Ay, part 'em now they are dead. Farewell, farewell.

 Exit.

 Enter [FERNEZE, *the*] *Governor,* KATHARINE
 [*and* ATTENDANTS].

FERNEZE. What sight is this? My Lodowick slain!   10
 These arms of mine shall be thy sepulchre.

KATHARINE. Who is this? My son Mathias slain!

FERNEZE. Oh Lodowick, hadst thou perished by the Turk,
 Wretched Ferneze might have venged thy death.

KATHARINE. Thy son slew mine, and I'll revenge his death.

FERNEZE. Look, Katharine, look, thy son gave mine these
 wounds.

KATHARINE. Oh leave to grieve me, I am grieved enough.

FERNEZE. Oh that my sighs could turn to lively breath,
 And these my tears to blood, that he might live.

KATHARINE. Who made them enemies?   20

FERNEZE. I know not, and that grieves me most of all.

KATHARINE. My son loved thine.

FERNEZE.   And so did Lodowick him.

KATHARINE. Lend me that weapon that did kill my son,
  And it shall murder me.

FERNEZE. Nay, Madam, stay; that weapon was my son's,
  And on that rather should Ferneze die.

KATHARINE. Hold, let's inquire the causers of their deaths,
  That we may venge their blood upon their heads.

FERNEZE. Then take them up, and let them be interred
  Within one sacred monument of stone,   30
  Upon which altar I will offer up
  My daily sacrifice of sighs and tears,
  And with my prayers pierce impartial Heavens,
  Till they [reveal] the causers of our smarts,
  Which forced their hands divide united hearts.
  Come, Katharine, our losses equal are;
  Then of true grief let us take equal share.

  Exeunt.

[III.iii]

Enter ITHAMORE.

ITHAMORE. Why, was there ever seen such villainy,
  So neatly plotted, and so well performed?
  Both held in hand, and flatly both beguiled.

  Enter ABIGAIL.

ABIGAIL. Why, how now, Ithamore, why laugh'st thou so?

ITHAMORE. Oh Mistress, ha, ha, ha!

ABIGAIL. Why, what ail'st thou?

ITHAMORE. Oh, my master!

ABIGAIL. Ha?

ITHAMORE. Oh Mistress! I have the bravest, gravest, secret,
subtle, bottle-nosed knave to my master, that ever gentle-
man had.   11

ABIGAIL. Say, Knave, why rail'st upon my father thus?

ITHAMORE. Oh, my master has the bravest policy.

ABIGAIL. Wherein?

ITHAMORE. Why, know you not?

ABIGAIL. Why, no.

ITHAMORE. Know you not of Mathias' and Don
Lodowick's disaster?

ABIGAIL. No, what was it?

ITHAMORE. Why, the devil invented a challenge, my master
writ it, and I carried it, first to Lodowick, and *imprimis* to
Mathias: 22
And then they met, [and] as the story says,
In doleful wise they ended both their days.

ABIGAIL. And was my father furtherer of their deaths?

ITHAMORE. Am I Ithamore?

ABIGAIL. Yes.

ITHAMORE. So sure did your father write, and I carry the
challenge.   30

ABIGAIL. Well, Ithamore, let me request thee this:
    Go to the new-made nunnery, and inquire
    For any of the friars of Saint Jaques,
    And say, I pray them come and speak with me.

ITHAMORE. I pray, Mistress, will you answer me to one
    question?

ABIGAIL. Well, Sirrah, what is 't?

ITHAMORE. A very feeling one: have not the nuns fine
    sport with the friars now and then?

ABIGAIL. Go to, Sirrah Sauce, is this your question? Get ye
    gone.

ITHAMORE. I will forsooth, Mistress.   40

    Exit.

ABIGAIL. Hard-hearted father, unkind Barabas,
    Was this the pursuit of thy policy,
    To make me show them favour severally,
    That by my favour they should both be slain?
    Admit thou lov'dst not Lodowick for his sire,
    Yet Don Mathias ne'er offended thee.
    But thou wert set upon extreme revenge,
    Because the Prior dispossessed thee once,
    And couldst not venge it but upon his son;
    Nor on his son but by Mathias' means;   50
    Nor on Mathias but by murdering me.
    But I perceive there is no love on earth,
    Pity in Jews, nor piety in Turks.
    But here comes cursed Ithamore with the friar.

    Enter ITHAMORE, *Friar* [JACOMO].

JACOMO. *Virgo, salve.*

ITHAMORE. When, duck you?

ABIGAIL. Welcome, grave friar. Ithamore, be gone.

   Exit [ITHAMORE].

  Know, holy Sir, I am bold to solicit thee.

JACOMO. Wherein?

ABIGAIL. To get me be admitted for a nun.   60

JACOMO. Why Abigail, it is not yet long since
   That I did labour thy admission,
   And then thou didst not like that holy life.

ABIGAIL. Then were my thoughts so frail and unconfirmed,
   And I was chained to follies of the world;
   But now experience, purchased with grief,
   Has made me see the difference of things.
   My sinful soul, alas, hath paced too long
   The fatal labyrinth of misbelief,
   Far from the Son that gives eternal life.   70

JACOMO. Who taught thee this?

ABIGAIL.   The Abbess of the house,
   Whose zealous admonition I embrace.
   Oh therefore, Jacomo, let me be one,
   Although unworthy, of that sisterhood.

JACOMO. Abigail, I will; but see thou change no more,
   For that will be most heavy to thy soul.

ABIGAIL. That was my father's fault.

JACOMO. Thy father's, how?

ABIGAIL. Nay, you shall pardon me. Oh Barabas,
   Though thou deservest hardly at my hands,
   Yet never shall these lips bewray thy life.   80

JACOMO. Come, shall we go?

ABIGAIL.   My duty waits on you.

   Exeunt.

Both females the same → actress....
coves—jew — Characters l the same

[III.iv]

Enter BARABAS *reading a letter.*

BARABAS. What, Abigail become a nun again?
   False and unkind! What, hast thou lost thy father?
   And, all unknown and unconstrained of me,
   Art thou again got to the nunnery?
   Now here she writes, and wills me to repent:
   Repentance? *Spurca!* What pretendeth this?
   I fear she knows ('tis so) of my device
   In Don Mathias' and Lodovico's deaths:
   If so, 'tis time that it be seen into;
   For she that varies from me in belief   10
   Gives great presumption that she loves me not;
   Or loving, doth dislike of something done.
   But who comes here?

[*Enter* ITHAMORE.]

                  Oh Ithamore, come near;
   Come near my love; come near, thy master's life,

My trusty servant, nay, my second life;
For I have now no hope but even in thee,
And on that hope my happiness is built.
When saw'st thou Abigail?

womanhood.

ITHAMORE. Today.   *Deceitful – womanly charms*

BARABAS. With whom?   20

ITHAMORE. A friar.

BARABAS. A friar? False villain, he hath done the deed.

ITHAMORE. How, Sir?

BARABAS. Why, made mine Abigail a nun.

ITHAMORE. That's no lie, for she sent me for him.

BARABAS. Oh unhappy day!   *Costume*
  False, credulous, inconstant Abigail!   *– purity – Virgin.*
  But let 'em go: and, Ithamore, from hence
  Ne'er shall she grieve me more with her disgrace;
  Ne'er shall she live to inherit aught of mine,   30
  Be blessed of me, nor come within my gates,
  But perish underneath my bitter curse,
  Like Cain by Adam for his brother's death.

ITHAMORE. Oh Master –

BARABAS. Ithamore, entreat not for her. I am moved,
  And she is hateful to my soul and me:
  And, 'less thou yield to this that I entreat,
  I cannot think but that thou hat'st my life.

ITHAMORE. Who, I, master? Why, I'll run to some rock,
  and throw myself headlong into the sea; why, I'll do
  anything for your sweet sake.   41

*Costume goes against what we see
but show what we expect to see.*

BARABAS. Oh trusty Ithamore; no servant, but my friend;
   I here adopt thee for mine only heir:
   All that I have is thine when I am dead;
   And whilst I live, use half; spend as myself.
   Here, take my keys – I'll give 'em thee anon.
   Go buy thee garments; but thou shalt not want.
   Only know this, that thus thou art to do:
   But first go fetch me in the pot of rice
   That for our supper stands upon the fire.   50

ITHAMORE. I hold my head, my master's hungry; I go, Sir.

   Exit.

BARABAS. Thus every villain ambles after wealth,
   Although he ne'er be richer than in hope.
   But hush 't!

   Enter ITHAMORE *with the pot.*

ITHAMORE. Here 'tis, Master.

BARABAS. Well said, Ithamore.
What, hast thou brought the ladle with thee too?

ITHAMORE. Yes, Sir; the proverb says, he that eats with the
   devil had need of a long spoon. I have brought you a ladle.

BARABAS. Very well, Ithamore, then now be secret;   61
   And for thy sake, whom I so dearly love,
   Now shalt thou see the death of Abigail,
   That thou mayst freely live to be my heir.

ITHAMORE. Why, Master, will you poison her with a mess
   of rice-porridge that will preserve life, make her round and
   plump, and batten more than you are aware?

BARABAS. Ay but, Ithamore, seest thou this?
    It is a precious powder that I bought
    Of an Italian in Ancona once,   70
    Whose operation is to bind, infect,
    And poison deeply, yet not appear
    In forty hours after it is ta'en.

ITHAMORE. How, Master?

BARABAS. Thus, Ithamore:
    This even they use in Malta here ('tis called
    Saint Jaques' Even) and then, I say, they use
    To send their alms unto the nunneries:
    Among the rest bear this, and set it there;
    There's a dark entry where they take it in,   80
    Where they must neither see the messenger
    Nor make inquiry who hath sent it them.

ITHAMORE. How so?

BARABAS. Belike there is some ceremony in't.
    There, Ithamore, must thou go place this pot:
    Stay, let me spice it first.

ITHAMORE. Pray do, and let me help you, Master. Pray let
    me taste first.

BARABAS. Prithee, do; what say'st thou now?

ITHAMORE. Troth, Master, I'm loath such a pot of pottage
    should be spoiled.   91

BARABAS. Peace, Ithamore, 'tis better so than spared.
    Assure thyself thou shalt have broth by the eye.
    My purse, my coffer, and myself is thine.

ITHAMORE. Well, Master, I go.

BARABAS. Stay, first let me stir it, Ithamore.
    As fatal be it to her as the draught
    Of which great Alexander drunk and died;
    And with her let it work like Borgia's wine,
    Whereof his sire the Pope was poisoned.   100
    In few, the blood of Hydra, Lerna's bane,
    The juice of hebon, and Cocytus' breath,
    And all the poisons of the Stygian pool,
    Break from the fiery kingdom; and in this
    Vomit your venom, and envenom her
    That like a fiend hath left her father thus.

ITHAMORE. What a blessing has he given't! Was ever pot of
    rice-porridge so sauced? What shall I do with it?

BARABAS. Oh my sweet Ithamore, go set it down;
    And come again so soon as thou hast done,   110
    For I have other business for thee.

ITHAMORE. Here's a drench to poison a whole stable of
    Flanders mares: I'll carry't to the nuns with a powder.

BARABAS. And the horse-pestilence to boot. Away.

ITHAMORE. I am gone:
    Pay me my wages, for my work is done.

    Exit.

BARABAS. I'll pay thee with a vengeance, Ithamore.

    Exit.

[III.v]

Enter [FERNEZE, *the*] *Governor,* BOSCO, KNIGHTS, BASHAW.

FERNEZE. Welcome, great Bashaw; how fares Calymath?
   What wind drives you thus into Malta road?

BASHAW. The wind that bloweth all the world besides,
   Desire of gold.

FERNEZE.   Desire of gold, great Sir?
   That's to be gotten in the Western Inde:
   In Malta are no golden minerals.

BASHAW. To you of Malta thus saith Calymath:
   The time you took for respite is at hand
   For the performance of your promise past,
   And for the tribute-money I am sent.   10

FERNEZE. Bashaw, in brief, shalt have no tribute here,
   Nor shall the heathens live upon our spoil:
   First will we raze the city walls ourselves,
   Lay waste the island, hew the temples down,
   And, shipping of our goods to Sicily,
   Open an entrance for the wasteful sea,
   Whose billows, beating the resistless banks,
   Shall overflow it with their refluence.

BASHAW. Well, Governor, since thou hast broke the league
   By flat denial of the promised tribute,   20
   Talk not of razing down your city walls,
   You shall not need trouble yourselves so far,
   For Selim-Calymath shall come himself,
   And with brass bullets batter down your towers,
   And turn proud Malta to a wilderness

For these intolerable wrongs of yours:
And so farewell.

[*Exit.*]

FERNEZE. Farewell.
And now, you men of Malta, look about,
And let's provide to welcome Calymath.   30
Close your portcullis, charge your basilisks,
And as you profitably take up arms,
So now courageously encounter them;
For by this answer broken is the league,
And naught is to be looked for now but wars,
And naught to us more welcome is than wars.

Exeunt.

[III.vi]

Enter two Friars [JACOMO *and* BARNARDINE].

JACOMO. Oh brother, brother, all the nuns are sick,
And physic will not help them; they must die.

BARNARDINE. The Abbess sent for me to be confessed.
Oh what a sad confession will there be!

JACOMO. And so did fair Maria send for me.
I'll to her lodging; hereabouts she lies.

Exit.

Enter ABIGAIL.

BARNARDINE. What, all dead save only Abigail?

ABIGAIL. And I shall die too, for I feel death coming.
    Where is the friar that conversed with me?

BARNARDINE. Oh he is gone to see the other nuns.   10

ABIGAIL. I sent for him, but seeing you are come,
    Be you my ghostly father: and first know,
    That in this house I lived religiously,
    Chaste, and devout, much sorrowing for my sins;
    But ere I came –

BARNARDINE. What then?

ABIGAIL. I did offend high Heaven so grievously
    As I am almost desperate for my sins;
    And one offence torments me more than all.
    You knew Mathias and Don Lodowick?   20

BARNARDINE. Yes, what of them?

ABIGAIL. My father did contract me to 'em both;
    First to Don Lodowick: him I never loved;
    Mathias was the man that I held dear,
    And for his sake did I become a nun.

BARNARDINE. So, say how was their end?

ABIGAIL. Both, jealous of my love, envied each other;
    And by my father's practice, which is there
    Set down at large, the gallants were both slain.

    [*Gives a paper.*]

BARNARDINE. Oh monstrous villainy!   30

ABIGAIL. To work my peace, this I confess to thee.

Reveal it not, for then my father dies.

BARNARDINE. Know that confession must not be revealed;
    The canon law forbids it, and the priest
    That makes it known, being degraded first,
    Shall be condemned, and then sent to the fire.

ABIGAIL. So I have heard; pray therefore keep it close.
    Death seizeth on my heart: ah, gentle Friar,
    Convert my father that he may be saved,
    And witness that I die a Christian.   40

    [*Dies.*]

BARNARDINE. Ay, and a virgin too; that grieves me most.
    But I must to the Jew and exclaim on him,
    And make him stand in fear of me.

    Enter first Friar [JACOMO].

JACOMO. Oh brother, all the nuns are dead; let's bury them.

BARNARDINE. First help to bury this; then go with me,
    And help me to exclaim against the Jew.

JACOMO. Why, what has he done?

BARNARDINE. A thing that makes me tremble to unfold.

JACOMO. What, has he crucified a child?   49

BARNARDINE. No, but a worse thing: twas told me in
shrift.
    Thou know'st 'tis death and if it be revealed.
    Come, let's away.

    Exeunt.

[IV.i]

Enter BARABAS, ITHAMORE. *Bells within.*

BARABAS. There is no music to a Christian's knell.
    How sweet the bells ring now the nuns are dead
    That sound at other times like tinkers' pans!
    I was afraid the poison had not wrought,
    Or though it wrought, it would have done no good,
    For every year they swell, and yet they live;
    Now all are dead, not one remains alive.

ITHAMORE. That's brave, Master; but think you it will not
    be known?

BARABAS. How can it, if we two be secret?

ITHAMORE. For my part, fear you not. 10

BARABAS. I'd cut thy throat, if I did.

ITHAMORE.   And reason too.
    But here's a royal monastery hard by;
    Good Master, let me poison all the monks.

BARABAS. Thou shalt not need, for now the nuns are dead
    They'll die with grief.

ITHAMORE. Do you not sorrow for your daughter's death?

BARABAS. No, but I grieve because she lived so long;
    An Hebrew born, and would become a Christian:
    Cazzo diavolo! 20

Enter the two Friars [JACOMO *and* BARNARDINE].

ITHAMORE. Look, look, Master, here come two religious
    caterpillars.

BARABAS. I smelt 'em ere they came.

ITHAMORE. God-a-mercy, nose; come, let's be gone.

BARNARDINE. Stay, wicked Jew; repent, I say, and stay.

JACOMO. Thou hast offended, therefore must be damned.

BARABAS. I fear they know we sent the poisoned broth.

ITHAMORE. And so do I, Master; therefore speak 'em fair.

BARNARDINE. Barabas, thou hast –

JACOMO. Ay, that thou hast –

BARABAS. True, I have money; what though I have?   30

BARNARDINE. Thou art a –

JACOMO. Ay, that thou art, a –

BARABAS. What needs all this? I know I am a Jew.

BARNARDINE. Thy daughter –

JACOMO. Ay, thy daughter –

BARABAS. Oh, speak not of her, then I die with grief.

BARNARDINE. Remember that –

JACOMO. Ay, remember that –

BARABAS. I must needs say that I have been a great usurer.

BARNARDINE. Thou hast committed –   40

BARABAS.   Fornication?
  But that was in another country,
  And besides, the wench is dead.

BARNARDINE. Ay, but Barabas, remember Mathias and
  Don Lodowick.

BARABAS. Why, what of them?

BARNARDINE. I will not say that by a forged challenge they
  met.

BARABAS [*aside*]. She has confessed, and we are both
    undone,
  My bosom inmates – (*Aside.*) but I must dissemble.
  Oh holy Friars, the burden of my sins
  Lie heavy on my soul; then pray you tell me,
  Is't not too late now to turn Christian?   50
  I have been zealous in the Jewish faith,
  Hard-hearted to the poor, a covetous wretch,
  That would for lucre's sake have sold my soul.
  A hundred for a hundred I have ta'en;
  And now for store of wealth may I compare
  With all the Jews in Malta: but what is wealth?
  I am a Jew, and therefore am I lost.
  Would penance serve for this my sin,
  I could afford to whip myself to death.

ITHAMORE. And so could I; but penance will not serve.   60

BARABAS. To fast, to pray, and wear a shirt of hair,
  And on my knees creep to Jerusalem.
  Cellars of wine, and sollars full of wheat,
  Warehouses stuffed with spices and with drugs,
  Whole chests of gold in bullion and in coin,

Besides I know not how much weight in pearl,
Orient and round, have I within my house;
At Alexandria, merchandise unsold;
But yesterday two ships went from this town,
Their voyage will be worth ten thousand crowns.   70
In Florence, Venice, Antwerp, London, Seville,
Frankfurt, Lubeck, Moscow, and where not,
Have I debts owing; and in most of these
Great sums of money lying in the banco.
All this I'll give to some religious house,
So I may be baptized and live therein.

JACOMO. Oh good Barabas, come to our house.

BARNARDINE. Oh no, good Barabas, come to our house.
And Barabas, you know –

BARABAS. I know that I have highly sinned: 80
You shall convert me, you shall have all my wealth.

JACOMO. Oh Barabas, their laws are strict.

BARABAS. I know they are; and I will be with you.

BARNARDINE. They wear no shirts, and they go barefoot too.

BARABAS. Then 'tis not for me; and I am resolved
You shall confess me, and have all my goods.

JACOMO. Good Barabas, come to me.

BARABAS You see I answer him, and yet he stays;
Rid him away, and go you home with me.

BARNARDINE. I'll be with you tonight.   90

BARABAS. Come to my house at one o'clock this night.

JACOMO. You hear your answer, and you may be gone.

BARNARDINE. Why go, get you away.

JACOMO. I will not go for thee.

BARNARDINE. Not? Then I'll make thee, rogue.

JACOMO. How, dost call me rogue?

Fight.

ITHAMORE. Part 'em, Master, part 'em.

BARABAS. This is mere frailty, Brethren, be content.
Friar Barnardine, go you with Ithamore.
[*Aside to* ITHAMORE.] You know my mind.   .   99

ITHAMORE.   Let me alone with him.

JACOMO. Why does he go to thy house? Let him be gone.

BARABAS. I'll give him something, and so stop his mouth.

Exit [ITHAMORE *with* BARNARDINE].

I never heard of any man but he
Maligned the order of the Jacobins;
But do you think that I believe his words?
Why, Brother, you converted Abigail;
And I am bound in charity to requite it,
And so I will. Oh Jacomo, fail not, but come.

JACOMO. But Barabas, who shall be your godfathers?
For presently you shall be shrived.   110

BARABAS. Marry, the Turk shall be one of my godfathers,
But not a word to any of your covent.

JACOMO. I warrant thee, Barabas.

Exit.

BARABAS. So, now the fear is past, and I am safe;
    For he that shrived her is within my house.
    What if I murdered him ere Jacomo comes?
    Now I have such a plot for both their lives
    As never Jew nor Christian knew the like:
    One turned my daughter, therefore he shall die;
    The other knows enough to have my life,   120
    Therefore 'tis not requisite he should live.
    But are not both these wise men to suppose
    That I will leave my house, my goods, and all,
    To fast and be well whipped? I'll none of that.
    Now Friar Barnardine, I come to you;
    I'll feast you, lodge you, give you fair words,
    And after that, I and my trusty Turk –
    No more but so: it must and shall be done.

Enter ITHAMORE.

    Ithamore, tell me, is the friar asleep?

ITHAMORE. Yes; and I know not what the reason is,   130
    Do what I can, he will not strip himself,
    Nor go to bed, but sleeps in his own clothes.
    I fear me he mistrusts what we intend.

BARABAS. No, tis an order which the friars use:
    Yet if he knew our meanings, could he 'scape?

ITHAMORE. No, none can hear him, cry he ne'er so loud.

BARABAS. Why, true; therefore did I place him there:
    The other chambers open towards the street.

ITHAMORE. You loiter, Master; wherefore stay we thus?

Oh how I long to see him shake his heels! 140

BARABAS. Come on, Sirrah, off with your girdle; make a
handsome noose. Friar, awake.

BARNARDINE. What, do you mean to strangle me?

ITHAMORE. Yes, 'cause you use to confess.

BARABAS. Blame not us, but the proverb: 'Confess and be
hanged.' Pull hard.

BARNARDINE. What, will you have my life?

BARABAS. Pull hard, I say. You would have had my goods.

ITHAMORE. Ay, and our lives too, therefore pull amain.
'Tis neatly done, Sir; here's no print at all. 150

BARABAS. Then is it as it should be. Take him up.

ITHAMORE. Nay, Master, be ruled by me a little. So, let
him lean upon his staff. Excellent! He stands as if he were
begging of bacon.

BARABAS. Who would not think but that this friar lived?
What time o'night is't now, sweet Ithamore?

ITHAMORE. Towards one.

BARABAS. Then will not Jacomo be long from hence.

[*Exeunt.*]

Enter JACOMO.

JACOMO. This is the hour wherein I shall proceed.
Oh happy hour, wherein I shall convert 160
An infidel, and bring his gold into our treasury!
But soft, is not this Barnardine? It is;

And understanding I should come this way,
Stands here o'purpose, meaning me some wrong,
And intercept my going to the Jew.
Barnardine –
Wilt thou not speak? Thou think'st I see thee not.
Away, I'd wish thee, and let me go by:
No, wilt thou not? Nay then, I'll force my way;
And see, a staff stands ready for the purpose.   170
As thou lik'st that, stop me another time.

Strike him, he falls. Enter BARABAS [*and* ITHAMORE].

BARABAS. Why, how now, Jacomo, what hast thou done?

JACOMO. Why, stricken him that would have struck at me.

BARABAS. Who is it? Barnardine? Now, out, alas, he is slain.

ITHAMORE. Ay, Master, he's slain; look how his brains drop
out on's nose.

JACOMO. Good Sirs, I have done't: but nobody knows it but
you two; I may escape.

BARABAS. So might my man and I hang with you for
company.

ITHAMORE. No, let us bear him to the magistrates.   180

JACOMO. Good Barabas, let me go.

BARABAS. No, pardon me, the law must have his course.
I must be forced to give in evidence
That being importuned by this Barnardine
To be a Christian, I shut him out,
And there he sat. Now I, to keep my word,
And give my goods and substance to your house,

Was up thus early, with intent to go
Unto your friary, because you stayed.   189

ITHAMORE. Fie upon 'em! Master, will you turn Christian,
   when holy friars turn devils and murder one another?

BARABAS. No, for this example I'll remain a Jew.
   Heaven bless me! What, a friar a murderer?
   When shall you see a Jew commit the like?

ITHAMORE. Why, a Turk could ha' done no more.

BARABAS. Tomorrow is the sessions; you shall to it.
   Come Ithamore, let's help to take him hence.

JACOMO. Villains, I am a sacred person; touch me not.

BARABAS. The law shall touch you, we'll but lead you, we.
   'Las, I could weep at your calamity.   200
   Take in the staff too, for that must be shown:
   Law wills that each particular be known.

   Exeunt.

[IV.ii]

Enter Courtesan [BELLAMIRA] *and* PILIA-BORZA.

BELLAMIRA. Pilia-Borza, didst thou meet with Ithamore?

PILIA-BORZA. I did.

BELLAMIRA. And didst thou deliver my letter?

PILIA-BORZA. I did.

BELLAMIRA. And what think'st thou? Will he come?

PILIA-BORZA. I think so, and yet I cannot tell; for at the reading of the letter, he looked like a man of another world.

BELLAMIRA. Why so?

PILIA-BORZA. That such a base slave as he should be saluted by such a tall man as I am, from such a beautiful dame as you.   11

BELLAMIRA. And what said he?

PILIA-BORZA. Not a wise word; only gave me a nod, as who should say, 'Is it even so?'; and so I left him, being driven to a non-plus at the critical aspect of my terrible countenance.

BELLAMIRA. And where didst meet him?

PILIA-BORZA. Upon mine own freehold, within forty foot of the gallows, conning his neck-verse, I take it, looking of a friar's execution; whom I saluted with an old hempen proverb, *Hodie tibi, cras mihi*, and so I left him to the mercy of the hangman; but the exercise being done, see where he comes.   23

Enter ITHAMORE.

ITHAMORE. I never knew a man take his death so patiently as this friar. He was ready to leap off ere the halter was about his neck; and when the hangman had put on his hempen tippet, he made such haste to his prayers as if he had had another cure to serve. Well, go whither he will, I'll be none of his followers in haste. And now I think on't, going to the execution, a fellow met me with a muschatoes

like a raven's wing, and a dagger with a hilt like a warming-
pan, and he gave me a letter from one Madam Bellamira,
saluting me in such sort as if he had meant to make clean
my boots with his lips. The effect was, that I should come
to her house. I wonder what the reason is; it may be she
sees more in me than I can find in myself; for she writes
further, that she loves me ever since she saw me, and who
would not requite such love? Here's her house; and here
she comes, and now would I were gone! I am not worthy
to look upon her.

PILIA-BORZA. This is the gentleman you writ to.   40

ITHAMORE. 'Gentleman'? He flouts me: what gentry can
be in a poor Turk of tenpence? I'll be gone.

BELLAMIRA. Is't not a sweet-faced youth, Pilia?

ITHAMORE. Again, 'sweet youth'; did not you, Sir, bring
the sweet youth a letter?

PILIA-BORZA. I did, Sir, and from this gentlewoman, who,
as myself and the rest of the family, stand or fall at your
service.

BELLAMIRA. Though woman's modesty should hale me
back, I can withhold no longer; welcome, sweet love.   49

ITHAMORE. Now am I clean, or rather foully, out of the
way.

BELLAMIRA. Whither so soon?

ITHAMORE. I'll go steal some money from my master to
make me handsome. Pray pardon me; I must go see a ship
discharged.

BELLAMIRA. Canst thou be so unkind to leave me thus?

PILIA-BORZA. And ye did but know how she loves you, Sir.

ITHAMORE. Nay, I care not how much she loves me. Sweet Allamira, would I had my master's wealth for thy sake!

PILIA-BORZA. And you can have it, Sir, and if you please.

ITHAMORE. If 'twere above ground, I could and would have it; but he hides and buries it up as partridges do their eggs, under the earth.   62

PILIA-BORZA. And is 't not possible to find it out?

ITHAMORE. By no means possible.

BELLAMIRA [aside to PILIA-BORZA]. What shall we do with this base villain, then?

PILIA-BORZA. Let me alone; do but you speak him fair: – But you know some secrets of the Jew, which, if they were revealed, would do him harm.

ITHAMORE. Ay, and such as – go to, no more! I'll make him send me half he has, and glad he 'scapes so too. Pen and ink: I'll write unto him; we'll have money straight.   71

PILIA-BORZA. Send for a hundred crowns at least.

ITHAMORE. Ten hundred thousand crowns.

He writes.

'Master Barabas – '

PILIA-BORZA. Write not so submissively, but threatening him.

ITHAMORE. 'Sirrah Barabas, send me a hundred crowns.'

PILIA-BORZA. Put in two hundred at least.

ITHAMORE. 'I charge thee send me three hundred by this
    bearer, and this shall be your warrant: if you do not – no
    more but so.'   80

PILIA-BORZA. Tell him you will confess.

ITHAMORE. 'Otherwise I'll confess all.' Vanish, and return
    in a twinkle.

PILIA-BORZA. Let me alone; I'll use him in his kind.

    [*Exit.*]

ITHAMORE. Hang him Jew!

BELLAMIRA. Now, gentle Ithamore, lie in my lap.
    Where are my maids? Provide a running banquet;
    Send to the merchant, bid him bring me silks;
    Shall Ithamore my love go in such rags?

ITHAMORE. And bid the jeweller come hither too.   90

BELLAMIRA. I have no husband, sweet; I'll marry thee.

ITHAMORE. Content: but we will leave this paltry land,
    And sail from hence to Greece, to lovely Greece.
    I'll be thy Jason, thou my golden fleece;
    Where painted carpets o'er the meads are hurled,
    And Bacchus' vineyards overspread the world;
    Where woods and forests go in goodly green;
    I'll be Adonis, thou shalt be Love's Queen;
    The meads, the orchards, and the primrose lanes,
    Instead of sedge and reed, bear sugar-canes: 100
    Thou in those groves, by Dis above,
    Shalt live with me and be my love.

BELLAMIRA. Whither will I not go with gentle Ithamore?

Enter PILIA-BORZA.

ITHAMORE. How now? Hast thou the gold?

PILIA-BORZA. Yes.

ITHAMORE. But came it freely? Did the cow give down her milk freely?

PILIA-BORZA. At reading of the letter, he stared and stamped, and turned aside. I took him by the beard, and looked upon him thus; told him he were best to send it. Then he hugged and embraced me.   111

ITHAMORE. Rather for fear than love.

PILIA-BORZA. Then like a Jew he laughed and jeered, and told me he loved me for your sake, and said what a faithful servant you had been.

ITHAMORE. The more villain he to keep me thus: here's goodly 'parel, is there not?

PILIA-BORZA. To conclude, he gave me ten crowns.

ITHAMORE. But ten? I'll not leave him worth a grey groat. Give me a ream of paper: we'll have a kingdom of gold for't.   121

PILIA-BORZA. Write for five hundred crowns.

ITHAMORE. 'Sirrah Jew, as you love your life, send me five hundred crowns, and give the bearer a hundred.' Tell him I must have't.

PILIA-BORZA. I warrant your worship shall have't.

ITHAMORE. And if he ask why I demand so much, tell him
I scorn to write a line under a hundred crowns.

PILIA-BORZA. You'd make a rich poet, Sir. I am gone.

Exit.

ITHAMORE. Take thou the money; spend it for my sake.

BELLAMIRA. Tis not thy money, but thyself I weigh.   131
Thus Bellamira esteems of gold;

[*Throws it aside.*]

But thus of thee.

Kisses him.

ITHAMORE. That kiss again; she runs division of my lips.
What an eye she casts on me! It twinkles like a star.

BELLAMIRA. Come my dear love, let's in and sleep
together.

ITHAMORE. Oh, that ten thousand nights were put in one,
that we might sleep seven years together afore we wake!

BELLAMIRA. Come, amorous wag, first banquet, and then
sleep.

[*Exeunt.*]

[IV.iii]

Enter BARABAS, *reading a letter.*

BARABAS. 'Barabas, send me three hundred crowns' –

Plain Barabas! Oh that wicked courtesan!
He was not wont to call me Barabas –
'Or else I will confess' – ay, there it goes:
But, if I get him, *coupe de gorge* for that.
He sent a shaggy, tottered, staring slave,
That when he speaks, draws out his grizzly beard,
And winds it twice or thrice about his ear;
Whose face has been a grindstone for men's swords;
His hands are hacked, some fingers cut quite off,   10
Who when he speaks, grunts like a hog, and looks
Like one that is employed in catzery
And crossbiting; such a rogue
As is the husband to a hundred whores:
And I by him must send three hundred crowns!
Well, my hope is, he will not stay there still;
And when he comes – Oh, that he were but here!

Enter PILIA-BORZA.

PILIA-BORZA. Jew, I must ha' more gold.

BARABAS. Why, want'st thou any of thy tale?   19

PILIA-BORZA. No, but three hundred will not serve his turn.

BARABAS. Not serve his turn, Sir?

PILIA-BORZA. No, Sir; and therefore I must have five
    hundred more.

BARABAS. I'll rather –

PILIA-BORZA. Oh, good words, Sir, and send it you were
    best; see, there's his letter.

BARABAS. Might he not as well come as send? Pray, bid him
    come and fetch it: what he writes for you, ye shall have straight.

PILIA-BORZA. Ay, and the rest too, or else –   30

BARABAS [*aside*]. I must make this villain away – Please you
dine with me, Sir, and you shall be most heartily (*Aside.*)
poisoned.

PILIA-BORZA. No, God-a-mercy; shall I have these crowns?

BARABAS. I cannot do it; I have lost my keys.

PILIA-BORZA. Oh, if that be all, I can pick ope your locks.

BARABAS. Or climb up to my counting-house window: you
know my meaning.

PILIA-BORZA. I know enough, and therefore talk not to me
of your counting-house; the gold, or know, Jew, it is in my
power to hang thee.   41

BARABAS. I am betrayed.
'Tis not five hundred crowns that I esteem;
I am not moved at that: this angers me,
That he who knows I love him as myself
Should write in this imperious vein. Why Sir,
You know I have no child, and unto whom
Should I leave all, but unto Ithamore?

PILIA-BORZA. Here's many words, but no crowns: the
crowns!

BARABAS. Commend me to him, Sir, most humbly,   50
And unto your good mistress as unknown.

PILIA-BORZA. Speak, shall I have 'em, Sir?

BARABAS. Sir, here they are.
Oh, that I should part with so much gold!
Here, take 'em, fellow, with as good a will –

[*Aside.*] As I would see thee hanged. – Oh, love stops my
    breath!
Never loved man servant as I do Ithamore.

PILIA-BORZA. I know it, Sir.

BARABAS. Pray when, Sir, shall I see you at my house?   59

PILIA-BORZA. Soon enough to your cost, Sir. Fare you well.

Exit.

BARABAS. Nay to thine own cost, villain, if thou com'st.
    Was ever Jew tormented as I am?
    To have a shag-rag knave to come [demand]
    Three hundred crowns, and then five hundred crowns!
    Well, I must seek a means to rid 'em all,
    And presently; for in his villainy
    He will tell all he knows, and I shall die for't.
    I have it.
    I will in some disguise go see the slave,
    And how the villain revels with my gold.

Exit.

[IV.iv]

Enter Courtesan [BELLAMIRA], ITHAMORE, PILIA-BORZA.

BELLAMIRA. I'll pledge thee, love, and therefore drink it
    off.

ITHAMORE. Say'st thou me so? Have at it! And, do you
    hear?

[*Whispers to her.*]

BELLAMIRA. Go to, it shall be so.

ITHAMORE. Of that condition I will drink it up: here's to
    thee.

BELLAMIRA. Nay, I'll have all or none.

ITHAMORE. There, if thou lov'st me, do not leave a drop.

BELLAMIRA. Love thee? Fill me three glasses.

ITHAMORE. Three and fifty dozen: I'll pledge thee.

PILIA-BORZA. Knavely spoke, and like a knight-at-arms.

ITHAMORE. Hey, *Rivo Castiliano!* A man's a man.   10

BELLAMIRA. Now to the Jew.

ITHAMORE. Ha to the Jew; and send me money you were
    best.

PILIA-BORZA. What wouldst thou do, if he should send
    thee none?

ITHAMORE. Do nothing. But I know what I know: he's a
    murderer.

BELLAMIRA. I had not thought he had been so brave a
    man.

ITHAMORE. You knew Mathias and the Governor's son: he
    and I killed 'em both, and yet never touched 'em.

PILIA-BORZA. Oh bravely done!   20

ITHAMORE. I carried the broth that poisoned the nuns;
    and he and I, snicle hand too fast, strangled a friar.

BELLAMIRA. You two alone?

ITHAMORE. We two; and 'twas never known, nor never shall be for me.

PILIA-BORZA [*aside to* BELLAMIRA]. This shall with me unto the Governor.

BELLAMIRA [*aside to* PILIA-BORZA]. And fit it should: but first let's ha' more gold.
Come, gentle Ithamore, lie in my lap.

ITHAMORE. Love me little, love me long: let music rumble,
Whilst I in thy incony lap do tumble.   30

Enter BARABAS *with a lute, disguised.*

BELLAMIRA. A French musician! Come, let's hear your skill.

BARABAS. Must tuna my lute for sound, twang twang first.

ITHAMORE. Wilt drink, Frenchman? Here's to thee with a – pox on this drunken hiccup!

BARABAS. *Gramercy, Monsieur.*

BELLAMIRA. Prithee, Pilia-Borza, bid the fiddler give me the posy in his hat there.

PILIA-BORZA. Sirrah, you must give my mistress your posy.

BARABAS. *A votre commandement, Madame.*   39

BELLAMIRA. How sweet, my Ithamore, the flowers smell!

ITHAMORE. Like thy breath, sweetheart; no violet like 'em.

PILIA-BORZA. Foh! Methinks they stink like a hollyhock.

BARABAS [*aside*]. So, now I am revenged upon 'em all.

The scent thereof was death; I poisoned it.

ITHAMORE. Play, fiddler, or I'll cut your cat's guts into chitterlings.

BARABAS. *Pardonnez moi*, be no in tune yet; so, now, now all be in.

ITHAMORE. Give him a crown, and fill me out more wine.

PILIA-BORZA. There's two crowns for thee; play.   50

BARABAS (*aside*). How liberally the villain gives me mine own gold!

[*He plays.*]

PILIA-BORZA. Methinks he fingers very well.

BARABAS (*aside*). So did you when you stole my gold.

PILIA-BORZA. How swift he runs.

BARABAS (*aside*). You run swifter when you threw my gold out of my window.

BELLAMIRA. Musician, hast been in Malta long?

BARABAS. Two, three, four month, *Madame*.

ITHAMORE. Dost not know a Jew, one Barabas?   60

BARABAS. Very mush, *Monsieur*, you no be his man?

PILIA-BORZA. His man?

ITHAMORE. I scorn the peasant: tell him so.

BARABAS [*aside*]. He knows it already.

ITHAMORE. 'Tis a strange thing of that Jew: he lives upon pickled grasshoppers and sauced mushrumps.

BARABAS (*aside*). What a slave's this! The Governor feeds
  not as I do.

ITHAMORE. He never put on clean shirt since he was
  circumcised.

BARABAS (*aside*). Oh rascal! I change myself twice a day.   70

ITHAMORE. The hat he wears, Judas left under the elder
  when he hanged himself.

BARABAS (*aside*). 'Twas sent me for a present from the Great
  Cham.

PILIA-BORZA. A masty slave he is. Whither now, fiddler?

BARABAS. *Pardonnez moi, Monsieur*, we be no well.

  Exit.

PILIA-BORZA. Farewell, fiddler. One letter more to the Jew.

BELLAMIRA. Prithee sweet love, one more, and write it
  sharp.

ITHAMORE. No, I'll send by word of mouth now. Bid him
  deliver thee a thousand crowns, by the same token that the
  nuns loved rice, that Friar Barnardine slept in his own
  clothes. Any of 'em will do it.   82

PILIA-BORZA. Let me alone to urge it now I know the
  meaning.

ITHAMORE. The meaning has a meaning. Come, let's in:
  To undo a Jew is charity, and not sin.

  Exeunt.

[V.i]

Enter [FERNEZE, *the*] *Governor,* KNIGHTS, *Martin del*
BOSCO [*and* OFFICERS].

FERNEZE. Now, Gentlemen, betake you to your arms,
And see that Malta be well fortified;
And it behoves you to be resolute,
For Calymath, having hovered here so long,
Will win the town, or die before the walls.

1 KNIGHT. And die he shall, for we will never yield.

Enter Courtesan [BELLAMIRA *and*] PILIA-BORZA.

BELLAMIRA. Oh bring us to the Governor.

FERNEZE, Away with her, she is a courtesan.

BELLAMIRA. Whate'er I am, yet Governor hear me speak.
I bring thee news by whom thy son was slain: 10
Mathias did it not; it was the Jew.

PILIA-BORZA. Who, besides the slaughter of these gentlemen,
Poisoned his own daughter and the nuns,
Strangled a friar, and I know not what
Mischief beside.

FERNEZE.   Had we but proof of this –

BELLAMIRA. Strong proof, my Lord: his man's now at my
          lodging
That was his agent; he'll confess it all.

FERNEZE. Go fetch him straight.

[*Exeunt* OFFICERS.]

I always feared that Jew.

Enter [OFFICERS *with*] BARABAS *and* ITHAMORE.

BARABAS. I'll go alone; dogs, do not hale me thus.   19

ITHAMORE. Nor me neither; I cannot outrun you,
Constable. Oh, my belly!

BARABAS. One dram of powder more had made all sure:
What a damned slave was I!

FERNEZE. Make fires, heat irons, let the rack be fetched.

[1] KNIGHT. Nay, stay, my Lord; 't may be he will confess.

BARABAS. Confess; what mean you, Lords? Who should
confess?

FERNEZE. Thou and thy Turk; 'twas you that slew my son.

ITHAMORE. Guilty, my Lord, I confess. Your son and
Mathias were both contracted unto Abigail: [he] forged a
counterfeit challenge.   30

BARABAS. Who carried that challenge?

ITHAMORE. I carried it, I confess; but who writ it? Marry,
even he that strangled Barnardine, poisoned the nuns and
his own daughter.

FERNEZE. Away with him, his sight is death to me.

BARABAS. For what? You men of Malta, hear me speak.
She is a courtesan, and he a thief,
And he my bondman; let me have law,

For none of this can prejudice my life.   39

FERNEZE. Once more, away with him; you shall have law.

BARABAS. Devils, do your worst. I live in spite of you.
As these have spoke, so be it to their souls! –
I hope the poisoned flowers will work anon.

[*Exeunt* OFFICERS *with* BARABAS, ITHAMORE;
BELLAMIRA, *and* PILIA-BORZA.]

Enter KATHARINE.

KATHARINE. Was my Mathias murdered by the Jew?
Ferneze, 'twas thy son that murdered him.

FERNEZE. Be patient, gentle Madam; it was he;
He forged the daring challenge made them fight.

KATHARINE. Where is the Jew? Where is that murderer?

FERNEZE. In prison, till the law has passed on him.

Enter OFFICER.

OFFICER. My Lord, the courtesan and her man are dead;   50
So is the Turk and Barabas the Jew.

FERNEZE. Dead?

OFFICER. Dead, my Lord, and here they bring his body.

BOSCO. This sudden death of his is very strange.

[*Enter* OFFICERS, *carrying* BARABAS *as dead*.]

FERNEZE. Wonder not at it, Sir; the Heavens are just.
Their deaths were like their lives; then think not of 'em.
Since they are dead, let them be buried.
For the Jew's body, throw that o'er the walls,

To be a prey for vultures and wild beasts.
So, now away and fortify the town.

Exeunt [except BARABAS].

BARABAS. What, all alone? Well fare, sleepy drink!   60
I'll be revenged on this accursed town;
For by my means Calymath shall enter in.
I'll help to slay their children and their wives,
To fire the churches, pull their houses down,
Take my goods too, and seize upon my lands.
I hope to see the Governor a slave,
And, rowing in a galley, whipped to death.

Enter CALYMATH, BASHAWS, TURKS.

CALYMATH. Whom have we there? A spy?   69

BARABAS. Yes, my good Lord, one that can spy a place
Where you may enter, and surprise the town.
My name is Barabas; I am a Jew.

CALYMATH. Art thou that Jew whose goods we heard were
     sold
For tribute-money?

BARABAS.   The very same, my Lord:
And since that time they have hired a slave, my man,
To accuse me of a thousand villainies.
I was imprisoned, but 'scaped their hands.

CALYMATH. Didst break prison?

BARABAS. No, no:
I drank of poppy and cold mandrake juice;   80
And being asleep, belike they thought me dead,
And threw me o'er the walls: so, or how else,

The Jew is here, and rests at your command.

CALYMATH. 'Twas bravely done. But tell me, Barabas,
    Canst thou, as thou report'st, make Malta ours?

BARABAS. Fear not, my Lord, for here, against the sluice,
    The rock is hollow, and of purpose digged
    To make a passage for the running streams
    And common channels of the city.
    Now, whilst you give assault unto the walls,   90
    I'll lead five hundred soldiers through the vault,
    And rise with them i'th'middle of the town,
    Open the gates for you to enter in,
    And by this means the city is your own.

CALYMATH. If this be true, I'll make thee Governor.

BARABAS. And if it be not true, then let me die.

CALYMATH. Thou'st doomed thyself. Assault it presently.

Exeunt.

[V.ii]

Alarms. Enter [CALYMATH *with*] TURKS, BARABAS;
    [FERNEZE, *the*] *Governor and* KNIGHTS [*with*] *prisoners.*

CALYMATH. Now vail your pride, you captive Christians,
    And kneel for mercy to your conquering foe.
    Now where's the hope you had of haughty Spain?
    Ferneze, speak; had it not been much better

To['ve] kept thy promise than be thus surprised?

FERNEZE. What should I say? We are captives and must
yield.

CALYMATH. Ay, villains, you must yield, and under Turkish
yokes
Shall groaning bear the burden of our ire.
And Barabas, as erst we promised thee,
For thy desert we make thee Governor;   10
Use them at thy discretion.

BARABAS.   Thanks, my Lord.

FERNEZE. Oh fatal day, to fall into the hands
Of such a traitor and unhallowed Jew!
What greater misery could Heaven inflict?

CALYMATH. 'Tis our command; and, Barabas, we give,
To guard thy person, these our Janizaries:
Entreat them well, as we have used thee.
And now, brave Bashaws, come; we'll walk about
The ruined town, and see the wrack we made.
Farewell brave Jew, farewell great Barabas.   20

Exeunt [CALYMATH *and* BASHAWS].

BARABAS. May all good fortune follow Calymath!
And now, as entrance to our safety,
To prison with the Governor and these
Captains, his consorts and confederates.

FERNEZE. Oh Villain, Heaven will be revenged on thee.

Exeunt [*except* BARABAS.]

BARABAS. Away, no more; let him not trouble me.

Thus hast thou gotten, by thy policy,
No simple place, no small authority:
I now am Governor of Malta; true,
But Malta hates me, and in hating me
My life's in danger; and what boots it thee,   30
Poor Barabas, to be the Governor,
Whenas thy life shall be at their command?
No, Barabas, this must be looked into;
And, since by wrong thou got'st authority,
Maintain it bravely by firm policy;
At least, unprofitably lose it not.
For he that liveth in authority,
And neither gets him friends nor fills his bags,
Lives like the ass that Æsop speaketh of
That labours with a load of bread and wine   40
And leaves it off to snap on thistle tops.
But Barabas will be more circumspect.
Begin betimes; Occasion's bald behind:
Slip not thine opportunity, for fear too late
Thou seek'st for much, but canst not compass it.
Within here!

Enter GOVERNOR *with a* GUARD.

FERNEZE. My Lord?

BARABAS.   Ay, 'Lord'; thus slaves will learn.
    Now, Governor – stand by there, wait within.

    [*Exeunt* GUARD.]

    This is the reason that I sent for thee:
    Thou seest thy life and Malta's happiness
    Are at my arbitrament; and Barabas   50

At his discretion may dispose of both.
Now tell me, Governor, and plainly too,
What think'st thou shall become of it and thee?

FERNEZE. This, Barabas: since things are in thy power,
    I see no reason but of Malta's wrack,
    Nor hope of thee but extreme cruelty.
    Nor fear I death, nor will I flatter thee.

BARABAS. Governor, good words, be not so furious.
    'Tis not thy life which can avail me aught;
    Yet you do live, and live for me you shall.   60
    And as for Malta's ruin, think you not
    'Twere slender policy for Barabas
    To dispossess himself of such a place?
    For sith, as once you said, within this isle,
    In Malta here, that I have got my goods,
    And in this city still have had success,
    And now at length am grown your Governor,
    Yourselves shall see it shall not be forgot;
    For as a friend not known but in distress,
    I'll rear up Malta now remediless.   70

FERNEZE. Will Barabas recover Malta's loss?
    Will Barabas be good to Christians?

BARABAS. What wilt thou give me, Governor, to procure
    A dissolution of the slavish bands
    Wherein the Turk hath yoked your land and you?
    What will you give me if I render you
    The life of Calymath, surprise his men,
    And in an out-house of the city shut
    His soldiers, till I have consumed 'em all with fire?
    What will you give him that procureth this?   80

FERNEZE. Do but bring this to pass which thou pretendest,
    Deal truly with us as thou intimatest,
    And I will send amongst the citizens,
    And by my letters privately procure
    Great sums of money for thy recompense:
    Nay more, do this, and live thou Governor still.

BARABAS. Nay, do thou this, Ferneze, and be free.
    Governor, I enlarge thee. Live with me;
    Go walk about the city, see thy friends.
    Tush, send not letters to 'em; go thy self,   90
    And let me see what money thou canst make.
    Here is my hand that I'll set Malta free.
    And thus we cast it: to a solemn feast
    I will invite young Selim-Calymath,
    Where be thou present, only to perform
    One stratagem that I'll impart to thee,
    Wherein no danger shall betide thy life,
    And I will warrant Malta free for ever.

FERNEZE. Here is my hand; believe me, Barabas,
    I will be there, and do as thou desirest.   100
    When is the time?

BARABAS.   Governor, presently.
    For Calymath, when he hath viewed the town,
    Will take his leave and sail toward Ottoman.

FERNEZE. Then will I, Barabas, about this coin,
    And bring it with me to thee in the evening.

BARABAS. Do so, but fail not. Now farewell, Ferneze.

    [*Exit* FERNEZE.]

    And thus far roundly goes the business:

Thus loving neither, will I live with both,
Making a profit of my policy;
And he from whom my most advantage comes,   110
Shall be my friend.
This is the life we Jews are used to lead;
And reason too, for Christians do the like.
Well, now about effecting this device:
First, to surprise great Selim's soldiers,
And then to make provision for the feast,
That at one instant all things may be done.
My policy detests prevention.
To what event my secret purpose drives,
I know; and they shall witness with their lives.   120

Exit.

[V.iii]

Enter CALYMATH, BASHAWS.

CALYMATH. Thus have we viewed the city, seen the sack,
And caused the ruins to be new repaired
Which with our bombards' shot and basilisk
We rent in sunder at our entry.
And now I see the situation,
And how secure this conquered island stands,
Environed with the Mediterranean sea
Strong countermured with other petty isles
And toward Calabria, backed by Sicily,   10
Where Syracusian Dionysius reigned,

Two lofty turrets that command the town.
I wonder how it could be conquered thus?

Enter a MESSENGER.

MESSENGER. From Barabas, Malta's Governor, I bring
    A message unto mighty Calymath:
    Hearing his sovereign was bound for sea,
    To sail to Turkey, to great Ottoman,
    He humbly would entreat your Majesty
    To come and see his homely citadel,
    And banquet with him ere thou leav'st the isle.

CALYMATH. To banquet with him in his citadel?   20
    I fear me, Messenger, to feast my train
    Within a town of war so lately pillaged,
    Will be too costly and too troublesome;
    Yet would I gladly visit Barabas,
    For well has Barabas deserved of us.

MESSENGER. Selim, for that, thus saith the Governor:
    That he hath in store a pearl so big,
    So precious, and withal so orient,
    As, be it valued but indifferently,
    The price thereof will serve to entertain   30
    Selim and all his soldiers for a month.
    Therefore he humbly would entreat your Highness
    Not to depart till he has feasted you.

CALYMATH. I cannot feast my men in Malta walls,
    Except he place his tables in the streets.

MESSENGER. Know, Selim, that there is a monastery
    Which standeth as an out-house to the town;
    There will he banquet them, but thee at home,

With all thy Bashaws and brave followers.

CALYMATH. Well, tell the Governor we grant his suit;   40
    We'll in this summer evening feast with him.

MESSENGER. I shall, my Lord.

    Exit.

CALYMATH. And now, bold Bashaws, let us to our tents,
    And meditate how we may grace us best
    To solemnize our Governor's great feast.

    Exeunt.

[V.iv]

Enter [FERNEZE, *the*] *Governor,* KNIGHTS, *del* BOSCO.

FERNEZE. In this, my countrymen, be ruled by me:
    Have special care that no man sally forth
    Till you shall hear a culverin discharged
    By him that bears the linstock, kindled thus;
    Then issue out and come to rescue me,
    For happily I shall be in distress,
    Or you released of this servitude.

1 KNIGHT. Rather than thus to live as Turkish thralls
    What will we not adventure?

FERNEZE. On then; be gone.

KNIGHTS.   Farewell, grave Governor.   10

    [*Exeunt.*]

[V.v]

Enter [BARABAS] *with a hammer, above, very busy* [*and* CARPENTERS].

BARABAS. How stand the cords? How hang these hinges, fast?
　　Are all the cranes and pulleys sure?

CARPENTER.   All fast.

BARABAS. Leave nothing loose, all levelled to my mind.
　　Why, now I see that you have art indeed.
　　There, Carpenters, divide that gold amongst you.
　　Go, swill in bowls of sack and muscadine;
　　Down to the cellar, taste of all my wines.

CARPENTER. We shall, my Lord, and thank-you.

　　Exeunt.

BARABAS. And if you like them, drink your fill and die;
　　For so I live, perish may all the world.　　　　　　　10
　　Now Selim-Calymath, return me word
　　That thou wilt come, and I am satisfied.

　　Enter MESSENGER.

　　Now, Sirrah, what, will he come?

MESSENGER. He will; and has commanded all his men
　　To come ashore, and march through Malta streets,
　　That thou mayst feast them in thy citadel.

BARABAS. Then now are all things as my wish would have 'em;
　　There wanteth nothing but the Governor's pelf;
　　And see, he brings it.

Enter FERNEZE.

                    Now, Governor, the sum.   20

FERNEZE. With free consent, a hundred thousand pounds.

BARABAS. Pounds say'st thou, Governor? Well, since it is no
    more,
  I'll satisfy myself with that; nay, keep it still,
  For if I keep not promise, trust not me.
  And Governor, now partake my policy:
  First, for his army, they are sent before,
  Entered the monastery, and underneath
  In several places are field-pieces pitched,
  Bombards, whole barrels full of gunpowder,
  That on the sudden shall dissever it   30
  And batter all the stones about their ears,
  Whence none can possibly escape alive.
  Now as for Calymath and his consorts,
  Here have I made a dainty gallery,
  The floor whereof, this cable being cut,
  Doth fall asunder, so that it doth sink
  Into a deep pit past recovery.
  Here, hold that knife; and when thou seest he comes,
  And with his Bashaws shall be blithely set,
  A warning-piece shall be shot off from the tower,   40
  To give thee knowledge when to cut the cord,
  And fire the house. Say, will not this be brave?

FERNEZE. Oh, excellent! Here, hold thee, Barabas;
  I trust thy word; take what I promised thee.

BARABAS. No, Governor, I'll satisfy thee first.
  Thou shalt not live in doubt of anything.
  Stand close, for here they come.

[FERNEZE *hides.*]

                              Why, is not this
A kingly kind of trade, to purchase towns
By treachery, and sell 'em by deceit?
Now tell me, worldlings, underneath the sun   50
If greater falsehood ever has been done.

Enter CALYMATH *and* BASHAWS.

CALYMATH. Come, my companion Bashaws, see, I pray,
　　How busy Barabas is there above
　　To entertain us in his gallery.
　　Let us salute him. Save thee, Barabas.

BARABAS. Welcome, great Calymath.

FERNEZE. How the slave jeers at him!

BARABAS. Will't please thee, mighty Selim-Calymath,
　　To ascend our homely stairs?

CALYMATH.   Ay, Barabas.
　　Come, Bashaws, attend.   60

FERNEZE [*coming forward*]. Stay, Calymath;
　　For I will show thee greater courtesy
　　Than Barabas would have afforded thee.

KNIGHT [*within*]. Sound a charge there!

A charge, the cable cut. A cauldron discovered [*into which*
BARABAS *falls. Enter* KNIGHTS *and del* BOSCO].

CALYMATH. How now, what means this?

BARABAS. Help, help me, Christians, help.

FERNEZE. See, Calymath, this was devised for thee.

CALYMATH. Treason, treason! Bashaws, fly.

FERNEZE. No, Selim, do not fly.
　　See his end first, and fly then if thou canst.　　　　70

BARABAS. Oh help me, Selim, help me, Christians.
　　Governor, why stand you all so pitiless?

FERNEZE. Should I in pity of thy plaints or thee,
　　Accursed Barabas, base Jew, relent?
　　No, thus I'll see thy treachery repaid,
　　But wish thou hadst behaved thee otherwise.

BARABAS. You will not help me, then?

FERNEZE. No, villain, no.

BARABAS. And villains, know you cannot help me now.
　　Then, Barabas, breathe forth thy latest fate,
　　And in the fury of thy torments strive　　　　80
　　To end thy life with resolution.
　　Know, Governor, 'twas I that slew thy son;
　　I framed the challenge that did make them meet.
　　Know, Calymath, I aimed thy overthrow;
　　And had I but escaped this stratagem,
　　I would have brought confusion on you all,
　　Damned Christians, dogs, and Turkish infidels.
　　But now begins the extremity of heat
　　To pinch me with intolerable pangs.
　　Die life, fly soul, tongue curse thy fill, and die.　　　　90

　　[*Dies.*]

CALYMATH. Tell me, you Christians, what doth this portend?

FERNEZE. This train he laid to have entrapped thy life.
　　Now, Selim, note the unhallowed deeds of Jews:

Thus he determined to have handled thee,
But I have rather chose to save thy life.

CALYMATH. Was this the banquet he prepared for us?
Let's hence, lest further mischief be pretended.

FERNEZE. Nay, Selim, stay, for since we have thee here,
We will not let thee part so suddenly.
Besides, if we should let thee go, all's one,   100
For with thy galleys couldst thou not get hence,
Without fresh men to rig and furnish them.

CALYMATH. Tush Governor, take thou no care for that.
My men are all aboard,
And do attend my coming there by this.

FERNEZE. Why, heard'st thou not the trumpet sound a charge?

CALYMATH. Yes, what of that?

FERNEZE.   Why, then the house was fired,
Blown up, and all thy soldiers massacred.

CALYMATH. Oh monstrous treason!

FERNEZE.   A Jew's courtesy.
For he that did by treason work our fall   110
By treason hath delivered thee to us.
Know therefore, till thy father hath made good
The ruins done to Malta and to us,
Thou canst not part; for Malta shall be freed,
Or Selim ne'er return to Ottoman.

CALYMATH. Nay rather, Christians, let me go to Turkey,
In person there to meditate your peace.
To keep me here will naught advantage you.

FERNEZE. Content thee, Calymath, here thou must stay,
    And live in Malta prisoner; for come all the world   120
    To rescue thee, so will we guard us now,
    As sooner shall they drink the ocean dry
    Than conquer Malta, or endanger us.
    So march away, and let due praise be given
    Neither to Fate nor Fortune, but to Heaven.

    [*Exeunt.*]

Finis

The Prologue to the Stage at the Cock-pit

We know not how our play may pass this stage,
But by the best of poets* in that age   * Marlowe
The Malta Jew had being and was made;
And he then by the best of actors† played: † Alleyn
In *Hero and Leander* one did gain
A lasting memory; in *Tamburlaine*,
This Jew, with others many, th'other won
The attribute of peerless, being a man
Whom we may rank with (doing no one wrong)
Proteus for shapes, and Roscius for a tongue,   10
So could he speak, so vary; nor is't hate
To merit in him‡ who doth personate   ‡ Perkins
Our Jew this day; nor is it his ambition
To exceed or equal, being of condition
More modest: this is all that he intends
(And that too, at the urgence of some friends)
To prove his best, and, if none here gainsay it,
The part he hath studied, and intends to play it.

Epilogue

In graving with Pygmalion to contend,
Or painting with Apelles, doubtless the end
Must be disgrace; our actor did not so:
He only aimed to go, but not out-go.
Nor think that this day any prize was played;
Here were no bets at all, no wagers laid;
All the ambition that his mind doth swell
Is but to hear from you (by me) 'twas well.

Glossary

Adonis Mythical youth with whom Venus ('Love's Queen') fell in love. He was killed by a wild boar in a hunting accident.

Agamemnon Greek general of the Trojan War. Having offended the goddess Artemis, he was forced to sacrifice his daughter, Iphigenia (here Iphigen) to placate her.

Alexander According to one version, Alexander the Great died after drinking wine poisoned by Antipater.

Apelles Greek painter.

Bacchus God of wine.

Bashaws Turkish soldiers.

Basilisks Type of canon.

Bien . . . es 'My gain is not good for everyone.'

Bombards Type of canon.

Borgia Reputed to have poisoned his father, Pope Alexander VI.

Britanie Britain.

Caire Cairo.

Candy Crete.

Catzery 'Employed in catzery', that is, 'working as a pimp.'

Cazzo diavolo 'By the devil's prick!'

Chitterlings Pig intestines prepared for eating, small sausages.

Cocytus In classical myth, one of the four rivers of Hades, the underworld.

Corpo di Dio 'By God's body!'

Coupe de gorge 'Cut his throat.'

Crossbiting   Double-dealing, swindling.

Culverin   A long cannon.

Dionysius   Ancient tyrant of Syracuse in Sicily.

Dis   Roman god of the underworld.

Draco   Legislator of ancient Athens renowned for his severity.

Ego . . . proximus   'I am always nearest to myself', meaning something like, 'I always put my own interests first.'

Field-pieces   Small portable cannon.

Guise   Henry, Duke of Guise (1550 – 88), fierce persecutor of Protestants.

Happily   Haply, perhaps (as at I. i. 117 and 160, V. iv. 6).

Hebon   Poisonous plant.

Hermoso . . . dineros   'Beautiful pleasure of money.'

Hodie . . . mihi   'Today, your turn, tomorrow, mine.'

Hydra   In Greek myth, many-headed monster with poisonous blood. Killed by Heracles.

Incony   Delicate, fine. Containing obscene pun on cony ('cunt').

Iphigen   See Agamemnon above.

Janizaries   Turkish soldiers.

Jason   According to Greek myth, Jason and the Argonauts succeeded in gaining the golden fleece.

Job   Old Testament figure who patiently endured the deprivation and suffering he was subjected to as a test by God.

Lerna   A marsh near Argos where the Hydra lived.

Linstock   Taper for lighting canon.

Maccabees   Books in the Apocrypha of the Bible.

Machevill   Niccolò Machiavelli (1469 – 1527), Italian political theorist. See introduction, page vii.

Masty   Fat, pig-like.

Morpheus   In Roman myth, the God of dreams and son of Somnus, god of sleep.

Ormus   City on Persian gulf famous for trading in gems.

Ottoman   Turkey.

Peter's chair   Papal throne.

Phalaris   Sicilian tyrant (BC 6th century) who executed his enemies by roasting them in a bull made of brass. After he was overthrown he met his fate in this instrument.

Philosopher's stone   Magic charm reputed to be capable of turning base metal into gold and endowing eternal youth. One of the main quests of alchemical research was to discover it.

Phoebus   God of light in Greek myth.

Plats   Spanish silver coins.

Portagues   Large gold coins from Portugal worth about £4.

Primus Motor   Prime mover, God.

Proteus   Sea god who could vary his outward form.

Pygmalion   Greek sculptor.

Rivo Castiliano   A toast meaning something like 'Let the liquor flow.'

Roscius   Famous Roman actor.

Spurca   'Filth!'

Stygian   Of the poisonous river Styx, principal river of the underworld in Grecian myth.

Ure   Use, practice.

Virgo, salve   'Greetings, maiden.'